the goose is **out**

OSHO

Extemporaneous talks given by Osho at the
OSHO International Meditation Resort, Pune, India

the goose is **out**

Zen in Action

Zen Cannot Be Studied – It Has to Be Lived

OSHO

This book is a series of original talks by Osho, given to a live audience. All
of Osho's talks have been published in full as books, and are also available
as original audio recordings. Audio recordings and the complete text
archive can be found via the online OSHO Library at
www.osho.com/library

OSHO is a registered trademark of OSHO International Foundation
www.osho.com/trademarks

OSHO MEDIA INTERNATIONAL
New York – Zurich – Mumbai
an imprint of
OSHO INTERNATIONAL
www.osho.com/oshointernational

Distributed by Publishers Group Worldwide
www.pgw.com

Library of Congress Catalog-In-Publication Data is available

Printed in India by Manipal Technologies Limited, Karnataka

ISBN 978-0-9836400-2-8
Also available as eBook ISBN 978-0-88050-364-8

contents

preface

Love.
That which is never lost cannot be found,
and to search for it is *absurd*.
But the moment this absurdity is understood all seeking stops
by itself
and that which is never lost is found!
That is why I say: *Seek and you will not find,*
because the *very seeking* is the barrier.
The search itself is the hindrance
because it creates the seeker, the ego, the illusion that I am.
And I am not.
Do not seek and you will find it: the *I-am-not-ness.*
This nothingness is the gate.
The Gateless gate.

Riko once asked Nansen
to explain to him the old problem of the goose in the bottle.
If a man puts a gosling into the bottle, he said, and feeds the
gosling through the bottle's neck until it grows and grows and
becomes a goose – and then there is simply no more room inside
the bottle, how can the man get it out without killing the goose or
breaking the bottle?
RIKO! shouted Nansen, and gave a great clap with his hands.
Yes master! said Riko with a start.
See! said Nansen. The goose is out!

Osho
A letter from *A Cup of Tea*

CHAPTER 1

the goose is out

The first question:

Osho,
Is the goose really out?

T he goose has never been in; the goose has always been out. It
is a Zen koan. First you have to understand the meaning of
Zen and the meaning of a koan.

Zen is not a religion, not a dogma, not a creed. Zen is not even a
quest, an inquiry; it is nonphilosophical. Fundamental to the Zen
approach is that all is as it should be, nothing is missing. This very
moment everything is perfect. The goal is not somewhere else – it
is here, it is now. Tomorrow doesn't exist. This very moment is the
only reality. Hence, in Zen there is no distinction between methods
and goals, between means and goals.

All the philosophies of the world and all the religions of the world
create duality. However they may go on talking about non-duality,
they create a split personality in man. That has been the greatest
calamity that has befallen humanity: all the do-gooders have created
a schizophrenic man. When you divide reality into means and goals

you divide man himself, because for man, man is the closest reality to man. His consciousness becomes split. He lives here, but not really; he is always somewhere else. He is always searching, always inquiring; never living, never being, always doing; getting richer, getting powerful, getting spiritual, getting holier, saintly – always more and more. And this constant hankering for more creates his tense, anguished state. Meanwhile he is missing all that is made available by existence. He is interested in the far away and godliness is close by. Man's eyes are focused on the stars and godliness is within him. Hence the most fundamental thing to understand about Zen is: the goose has never been in. Let me tell you the story of how this koan started:

A great philosophical official, Riko, once asked the strange Zen master, Nansen, to explain to him the old koan of the goose in the bottle.

"If a man puts a gosling into a bottle," said Riko, "and feeds him until he is full-grown, how can the man get the goose out without killing it or breaking the bottle?"

Nansen gave a great clap with his hands and shouted, "Riko!"

"Yes, Master," said the official with a start.

"See!" said Nansen, "the goose is out!"

It is only a question of seeing, it is only a question of becoming alert, awake, it is only a question of waking up. The goose is in the bottle if you are in a dream; the goose has never been in the bottle if you are awake. In the dream there is no way to take the goose out of the bottle. Either the goose will die or the bottle will have to be broken. Both alternatives are not allowed: neither has the bottle to be broken nor has the goose to be killed. Now, a fully-grown goose in a small bottle... How can you take it out? This is called a koan.

A koan is not an ordinary puzzle; it is not a puzzle because it cannot be solved. A puzzle is that which has a possibility of being solved; you just have to look for the right answer. You will find it – it only needs intelligence to find the answer to the puzzle, but a puzzle is not really insoluble.

A koan is insoluble, you cannot solve it, you can only *dissolve* it. And the way to dissolve it is to change the very plane of your being from dreaming to wakefulness. In the dream the goose is in the bottle and there is no way to bring it out of the bottle without breaking the bottle or killing the goose – in the dream. Hence, as far as the dream is concerned the puzzle is impossible; nothing can be done about it.

But there is a way out – which has nothing to do with the puzzle, remember. You have to wake up. That has nothing to do with the bottle and nothing to do with the goose either. You have to wake up. It has something to do with *you*. That's why Nansen did not answer the question.

Riko asked, "If a man puts a gosling into a bottle and feeds him until he is full-grown, how can the man get the goose out without killing it or breaking the bottle?"

Nansen didn't answer. On the other hand, he gave a great clap with his hands and shouted, "Riko!"

Now, this is not an answer to the question – this has nothing to do with the question at all – it is irrelevant, inconsistent. But it solves it; in fact, it dissolves it. The moment he shouted, "Riko!" the official with a start said, "Yes, Master," and the whole plane of his being is transformed by a simple strategy.

A master is not a teacher; he does not teach you, he simply devises methods to wake you up. That clap is a method, that clap simply brought Riko into the present. And it was so unexpected... When you are asking such a spiritual koan you don't expect the master to answer you with a loud clap and then shout, "Riko!"

Suddenly he is brought from the past, from the future. Suddenly for a moment he forgets the whole problem. Where is the bottle and where is the goose? There is only the master, in a strange posture, clapping and shouting for Riko. Suddenly the whole problem is dropped. He has slipped out of the problem without even knowing that he slipped out of it. He has slipped out of the problem as a snake slips out of its old skin. For a moment time has stopped. For a moment the clock has stopped. For a moment the mind has stopped. For a moment there is nothing. The master, the sound of the clap, and a sudden awakening. In that very moment the master says, "See! See, the goose is out!" It is dissolved.

A koan can only be dissolved but can never be solved. A puzzle can never be dissolved but can be solved. So remember, a koan is not a puzzle.

But when people who are accustomed to continuous thinking,

logical reasoning, start studying Zen, they take a false step from the very beginning. Zen cannot be studied; it has to be lived, it has to be imbibed – imbibed from a living master. It is a transmission beyond words, a transmission of the lamp. The lamp is invisible.

Now, anybody watching this whole situation – Riko asking a question, the master clapping and shouting – would not have found anything very spiritual in it, would not have found any great philosophy, may have become very frustrated. But something transpired, something which is not visible and can never be visible.

It happens only when the silence of the master penetrates the silence of the disciple. When two silences meet and merge; then immediately there is seeing. The master has eyes, the disciple has eyes, but the disciple's eyes are closed. A device is needed, some method, so that the disciple can open his eyes without any effort of his own. If he makes an effort he will miss the point, because who will make the effort?

Christmas Humphreys, one of the great lovers of Zen in the West, the founder of the Buddhist Society of England and the man who made Zen Buddhism very famous in the Western world, writes about this koan, and you will see the difference. He says:

"There is a method of taking the problem in flank, as it were. It will be nonsense to the rational-minded, but such will read no further. Those who read on will expect increasing nonsense; for sense, the suburban villas of rational thought, will soon be left behind. The mind will be free on the illimitable hills of its own inherent joy. Here, then, is the real solution to the problem of the opposites.

"Shall I tell it to you? Consider a live goose in a bottle. How to get it out without hurting the goose or breaking the bottle? The answer is simple – 'There, it is!'"

Now, the whole point is lost: it becomes philosophical. First, Christmas Humphreys thinks Zen is part of Buddhism; that assumption begins with a wrong door, with a wrong step. Zen has nothing to do with Buddhism. It certainly has something to do with the Buddha but nothing to do with Buddhism as such – just as Sufism has nothing to do with Islam, Hasidism has nothing to do with Judaism, Tantra has nothing to do with Hinduism. Yes, Tantra certainly has something to do with Shiva, and Sufism has something to do with

Mohammed, and Hasidism has something to do with Moses, but not with the traditions, not with the conventions, not with the theologies.

A Moses alive, a Mohammed alive, can transmit something which cannot be said, can show something which cannot be said, can create a certain vibe around him which can trigger enlightenment in many people, but without any explanation, without any logical proof.

Enlightenment is almost like a love affair. Just as you fall in love – you cannot rationalize it; it is below reason – in the same way that you fall into enlightenment. It is *above* reason: you fall above words.

There is a beautiful story of a master who was staying at a disciple's house. The disciple was a little worried about the master because his ways were strange, unexpected. He could do anything! He was almost thought to be mad. So not to create any trouble for the neighborhood – because in the night he might start dancing, singing, shouting, sermonizing to nobody and create a disturbance in the neighborhood – they put him in the basement and locked him up in the basement, so that even if he went and did something nobody would hear him. They closed all the windows, all the doors, and locked them.

In the middle of the night they were suddenly awakened. Somebody was rolling about on the roof with such a loud laughter that a great crowd had gathered all around and they were asking, "What is the matter?"

They rushed up; they found the master rolling on the roof. They asked, "What is the matter? How did you manage this? We locked you in the basement just to avoid such a scene!"

The master said, "That's why I am laughing. Suddenly I started falling upward. I cannot believe it myself! It has never happened before, falling upward!"

It is a beautiful story. Enlightenment is falling upward just as love is falling downward. But something is similar in both; the falling – unreasonable, unexplainable, inexpressible. Only those to whom it has happened know, and even when it has happened you cannot explain it to anybody to whom it has not yet happened.

Christmas Humphreys calls Zen "Zen Buddhism"; that is starting in the wrong direction from the very beginning. Zen is not Buddhism – the essential core of the heart of Buddha, certainly, but it is the essential core of Moses too, the essential core of Zarathustra too, Lao Tzu too. It is the essential core of all those who have become enlightened, of all those who have awakened from their dream, of all those who have seen that the goose is out, that the goose has never been in, that the problem is not a problem at all in the first place, hence no solution is needed.

Christmas Humphreys says, "There is a method of taking the problem in flank, as it were. It will be nonsense to the rational-minded..."

He himself is rational-minded; otherwise, it is not nonsense. Nonsense is something below sense. Zen is supra-sense, not nonsense; it is above sense. It is something far beyond the reaches of reason. Logic is a very ordinary game; anybody who has a little intelligence can play the game. The moment you go beyond logic then you enter into the world of Zen. It is not nonsense, it is supra-sense. His very use of the word *nonsense* shows a deep-down bias toward rationality.

He says: "...but such will read no further. Those who read on will expect increasing nonsense; for sense, the suburban villas of rational thought, will soon be left behind..."

They are not left behind, because if you leave something behind, you are on the same track. You have left a milestone behind but the road is the same, the path is not different. Maybe you have gone a mile ahead but your dimension has not changed. The difference is only of quantity, not of quality.

Reason is not only left behind, reason is transcended, surpassed. There is a difference, a great difference, a difference that makes the difference.

I have heard a story. It happened in the Second World War:

In a thick, primitive part of Burma, a small airplane was left by the army. They were in a hurry, they were retreating, and for some mechanical reason they could not manage to take it with them. The primitives found the plane; they could not understand what it was. They figured out that it must be some kind of bullock cart – that was the only possible thing for them to think; the bullock cart was the ultimate vehicle in their vision. So they started using the plane as a bullock cart, and they enjoyed it. It was the best bullock cart they had ever found!

Then somebody was passing by – a man who lived a little further away from the primitive tribe but was part of the tribe. He knew – he had experienced cars, trucks, buses. He said, "This is not a bullock cart, this is a car, and I know something about cars." So he fixed it, and they were immensely amazed that without horses, without bulls, the machine was working. It was such a toy! Every morning, every evening, they enjoyed just looking at it again and again from all sides, entering it, sitting in it; and because there were not many roads, even to go a few feet was a great excitement.

Then one day a pilot passed by the primitive forest and he said, "What are you doing? This is an airplane, it can fly!"

He took two primitives with him, and when they left the ground they could not believe it. This was absolutely beyond their imagination, beyond all their dreams. They used to think that only gods could fly; they had heard stories about gods flying in the sky. Yes, they had seen airplanes in the sky, but they had always believed they belonged to the gods.

Now, the same mechanism can be used as a bullock cart or as a car, but between the bullock cart and the car the distinction is only of quantity, not of quality. The moment the airplane takes off from the ground it changes. It's a plane: it surpasses the bullock cart and the car. It moves in a totally new dimension.

So reason is not left behind, reason is simply transcended. Hence, Christmas Humphreys called it "nonsense," "irrational." His thinking that reason had been left behind was still thinking in terms of rationality.

He says: "…and the mind will be free…"

Now, that is absolutely stupid: the mind will not be free. When you enter into the world of Zen there is no-mind. Zen is the equivalent of no-mind. It is not freedom of the mind, it is freedom *from* the mind – and there is a lot of difference, an unbridgeable difference. The *mind* is not free, *you* are free – of the mind. The mind is no longer there, free or unfree; the mind has simply ceased. You have gone through a new door which was always available to you, but you had never knocked on it – the door of being, the door of eternity.

Zen, the very word *Zen* comes from the Sanskrit word *dhyana*. *Dhyana* means meditation, but the word *meditation* does not carry its total significance. *Meditation* again gives you the feeling that mind is doing something: mind meditating, concentrating, contemplating, but mind is there. *Dhyana* simply means a state of no-mind, no concentration, no contemplation. It means, not meditation, but just a silence, a deep, profound silence where all thoughts have disappeared; where there is no ripple in the lake of consciousness; when the consciousness is functioning just like a mirror reflecting all that is – the stars, the trees, the birds, the people, all that is – simply reflecting it without any distortion, without any interpretation, without bringing in your prejudices. That's what your mind is: your prejudices, your ideologies, your dogmas, your habits.

Christmas Humphreys says: "...and the mind will be free on the illimitable hills of its own inherent joy."

This is *real* nonsense! First, "mind will be free." Mind can never be free. Freedom and mind never meet. Mind means bondage, mind is a prison. In the mind you live an encapsulated life, surrounded by all kinds of thoughts, theories, systems, philosophies, surrounded by the whole past of humanity, all kinds of superstitions – Hindu, Mohammedan, Christian, Buddhist, Jaina – political, social, economic, religious. Either your mind is made up of the bricks of the Bible, the Koran, the Gita, or maybe *Das Kapital* or the *Communist Manifesto*. You may have made your prison differently from others, you may have chosen a different architect, but the prison is the same. The architect can be Sigmund Freud, Karl Marx, Albert Einstein – you can choose. Prisons come in all shapes and all sizes – and the interior decoration is up to you. You can put beautiful paintings inside, you can carpet it wall to wall, you can paint it according to your likes and dislikes, you can make a few changes here and there, a window on the left or on the right, a curtain of this material or that, but a prison is a prison.

Mind as such is a prison, and everybody is living in the prison. Unless you get out of the prison you will never know what freedom is. Your prison can be very cozy, comfortable, convenient. It can be very well decorated; it can be golden, or studded with diamonds.... It will be difficult to leave it: you have worked so hard to create it, it is not going to be easy. But a prison is a prison; made of gold or made of mud, it makes no difference. You will never know the infinity of freedom; you will never know the beauty and the splendor of freedom; your splendor will remain imprisoned. You will never know what godliness is. You will never know that the goose is always out. You will live in all kinds of dreams. Howsoever beautiful they are, dreams are dreams, and sooner or later all dreams are shattered.

Mind is self-perpetuating. If one dream shatters it immediately creates another dream – in fact, it always keeps one ready. Before the old one is shattered it supplies you with a new one – a better dream, more refined, more sophisticated, more scientific, more technological – and again you are infatuated, again the desire arises: "Why not try it? Maybe other dreams have failed, but that does not necessarily mean that all dreams will fail. One may succeed." That hope goes on lingering, that hope keeps you running after dreams. And when death comes, one finds that one's whole life has been nothing but the same stuff as dreams are made of: "...a tale told by an idiot, full of sound and fury, signifying nothing." But this is how millions of people are living.

Christmas Humphreys says: "...and the mind will be free on the illimitable hills of its own inherent joy."

This shows that he never understood even a single dewdrop of the Zen experience. He became the propagator of Zen philosophy in the West, but not knowing what he was doing, not experiencing anything of what he was talking.

The mind cannot reach "the illimitable hills of its own inherent joy"; the mind has no inherent capacity for joy. The mind is the cause of all misery – the only cause, there is no other cause of misery. Hence mind knows nothing of joy. It only thinks about joy, and its thinking about joy is also nothing but an imagination against the suffering in which it lives.

If you ask the mind to define joy, its definition will be negative. It will simply say, "There will be no suffering, there will be no pain, there will be no death." But this is all negative definition; it says nothing about bliss, it simply speaks about painlessness. But the goal of painlessness is not of any worth. If you are without pain, will you find that life worth living, and for how long? If you have no illness that does not mean that you have the well-being of health; that is a totally different quality. A person may be medically fit, there may be nothing wrong as far as the diagnosis of the physician goes, but if he is not feeling an overflowing joy it is not health – an absence of disease perhaps, but not the presence of health. The absence of disease is not equivalent to the presence of health; that's a totally different phenomenon.

You may not be miserable; that does not mean that you are

blissful. You may be simply in limbo, neither blissful nor miserable. This is a far worse situation than being miserable, because the miserable person at least tries to get out of it. The person who lives in limbo, just on the boundary line, neither miserable nor blissful, cannot get out of misery because he is not in misery. He cannot enter into bliss because there is no push from behind; the misery is not hitting him hard enough for him to take a jump. He will remain stuck, stagnant.

Misery is a negative state, bliss is a positive state – but the mind knows only misery. The mind cannot know "the illimitable hills of its own inherent joy" because there is nothing in it. The mind is only a creation of society to help you perform your social duties efficiently. The mind is a strategy of the establishment to manipulate you, to enslave you, to keep you as unintelligent as possible, because the intelligent person is dangerous.

In the whole of the Bible there is not a single statement praising intelligence. It is full of all kinds of rubbish, but there is not a single statement in praise of intelligence. Superstition is praised, belief is praised, all kinds of stupid things are praised.

All the religions, organized religions, have been trying to make man a robot, a machine, and they have almost succeeded. That's why there are so few Buddhas, so few Jesuses. The reason is simple: societies, factories, the state, the church, the nation – they are in a deep conspiracy to destroy the small child, who is very vulnerable, delicate and helpless.

You can destroy him. And the basic strategy for destruction is to create a mind, impose a mind on him, so that he forgets his innermost qualities of joy. He forgets the innocence that he brought from the sources of existence; he forgets all that is beautiful and becomes only a cog in the wheel of society. He has to be a good servant, he has to be a good mechanic, he has to be a good stationmaster, a good professor, this and that, but he may not to be a divine being, he may not to function blissfully.

The society is very afraid of blissful people for the simple reason that bliss is such a tremendous experience that one can sacrifice one's life for it. But one cannot sacrifice one's bliss for anything else. One lives for bliss, one dies for bliss, once one has known what bliss is. Hence the blissful person is absolutely beyond the imprisoning forces of the society. The society can only rule those who are miserable, the church can only exploit those who are miserable.

Christmas Humphreys says: "Here, then, is the real solution to the problem of the opposites."

There is no "problem of the opposites." Opposites are not opposites, they are complements, hence there is no problem as such. Darkness and light are one phenomenon, two aspects of the same coin. Life and death are inseparable, you cannot separate them – how can you make them opposites? They are complements, they help each other. Hence, there is no problem, and there is no need for any solution.

Zen is not a solution to opposites, it is a transcendence. It is a higher vision, a bird's-eye view from where all dualities look stupid.

The most important thing that happened to the first man who walked on the moon was that he suddenly forgot that he was an American. Suddenly the whole earth was one, there were no boundaries, because there is no map drawn on the earth. The American continent, the African continent, the Asian continent, this country and that country all disappeared. He made no effort to put all the opposing camps together; there was not a Soviet Russia or an America, the whole earth was simply just one.

And the first words that were uttered by the American were, "My beloved earth!" This is transcendence. For a moment he had forgotten all conditionings: "My beloved earth!" Now the whole earth belonged to him.

This is what actually happens in a state of silence: the whole of existence is yours and all opposites disappear into each other, supporting, dancing with each other. It becomes an orchestra.

Christmas Humphreys says, "Shall I tell it to you? Consider…"

Now, see how small changes make great differences: "Shall I tell it to you? Consider…" This is the way philosophy moves, not Zen: consider… It is not a question of consideration – either you know or you don't know.

The master Nansen did not say, "Consider, now I will give a great clap. Consider, now I will shout, 'Riko!' and you have to say, 'Yes, Master!' Then I will say, 'See, the goose is out!'" Then the whole point would have been lost.

Just a few days ago in a *darshan* meeting in the evening I called Nirupa. She had broken one of her hands. She is one of my mediums, but now she cannot participate in the dancing. She was just sitting in the front row and I called her. For a moment she hesitated and everybody laughed, because what was she going to do with one hand? But Zen is done with one hand – the sound of one hand clapping! – and she did well. Of course, only I could hear the sound. The sound of one hand clapping – even when you are making a sound with two hands clapping the energy is one. Your left hand and your right hand are not two, they are joined in you. They are not opposites; they are complementary; they belong to one being.

All opposites belong to one being, and it is not a question of consideration. If you consider, you take all the juice out of the beautiful koan.

"Consider," he says, "a live goose in a bottle. How to get it out without hurting the goose or breaking the bottle?"

He cannot even say "without *killing* the goose" – a proper English-man! – "without hurting the goose or breaking the bottle." In fact, even to say "breaking the bottle," his heart must be breaking! "The answer is simple…"

It is not simple. In the first place, it is not an answer either. "There, it is out!" He has destroyed the whole beauty of the koan. But habits die very hard. It is just the way of thinking, the way of the mind.

The Pope was given a pair of red silk slippers with the initials T.I.F inscribed on them. When His Holiness asked what the letters stood for, he was told, "Toes in first."

You ask me: "Osho, is the goose really out?"

It has always been out, it has never been in. It is only a question of dreaming.

Wake up!

The second question:

Osho,
In the West I am a student of philosophy. Is there any love or wisdom in philosophy? I have not found them yet.

It is good that you have not found it yet. I hope that you will never find it, ever, because Germans tend to find it!

It is said philosophy is like a blind man searching on a dark night in a dark room for a black cat which is not there. But Germans find it!

They have given the greatest philosophers to the world: Immanuel Kant and Hegel and Fichte and Marx and Feuerbach and so on and so forth.

It is good that you say: "In the West I am a student of philosophy. Is there any love or wisdom in philosophy?"

Love is not possible at all, because philosophy means logic and logic cannot be loving. Logic is the foundation of science but not the foundation of life. Logic is applicable to dead things, to objects, because the basic method of logic is dissection. The moment you dissect something you kill it, so if you want to find life through logic you will never find it; the very method prohibits it.

You can cut a rose flower, you can dissect it, you can put all the ingredients separately into different bottles methodically labeled, but one thing will be missing: there will be no beauty to be found and no life to be found, no joy to be found, no dance of the rose flower in the wind, in the rain, in the sun; they will all be gone. There will be a few chemicals, but those chemicals are not the rose flower. Those chemicals were simply the situation in which the rose has appeared. They don't constitute the rose, they only constituted the situation for the appearance of the rose. If you take them away the rose disappears into its invisible world.

It is like dissecting a dancer – do you think you will find something like dance inside? You will find bones, you will find all kinds of nasty things, but you will not find a dance. You can cut the throat of a singer, but you will not find the song – and you had always believed that the song came from the throat! The throat is only a vehicle; the song comes from the beyond. The throat can be a good vehicle or a bad vehicle – that is a different matter – but it is only a vehicle. By dissecting the vehicle you cannot find that which was descending on it from the world of the beyond.

Love and logic never meet, *cannot* meet. Logic means the outward journey, love means the inward journey. Logic means dissection, love means finding the organic unity. Logic thinks in terms of the many, the multiple.

In fact, scientists should stop calling the universe "universe," they should call it "multiverse." "Universe" is a poetic name given by lovers; universe means one, *uni*. According to science it is not a universe, it is many, it is a multiverse. Only lovers know the unity, thinkers cannot know unity.

In the unity of the whole one finds love, and one finds wisdom. Wisdom is the shadow of love: wherever there is love there is wisdom. When love is alive there is dance, there is song, there is beauty; those are all the qualities of wisdom. If you think logic can give you wisdom then you will have to decide one thing very clearly, and that is that knowledge has to be taken as wisdom. Then logic can give you wisdom, but then knowledge becomes equivalent to, synonymous with, wisdom – and knowledge is *not* synonymous with wisdom. Knowledge is all borrowed, rubbish; you have gathered it from others.

Wisdom is the explosion of your own consciousness. Wisdom is intrinsic; it does not come from the outside, it explodes within you and spreads toward the outer world. It is like light radiating: you share it, you don't accumulate it. Knowledge has to be begged for, wisdom has to be shared. They are totally different dimensions.

Philosophy cannot give you love or wisdom, but it can go on giving you hope. If philosophy is the answer, it must have been a silly question.

Remember it, if you can find any answer through philosophy that simply proves one thing: that your question was silly. If the question is really significant, philosophy has no answer. You will have to look in a different direction. That direction I call Zen, that direction I call awakening – not theorizing, philosophizing, but becoming silent; not becoming more knowledgeable but dropping all knowledge, discarding it so that you can be empty, utterly empty. In emptiness there is clarity, there is cleanliness, there is purity, there is innocence, a child-like wonder and awe. And those are the moments of love and wisdom growing in you; they grow together. Knowledge and logic grow together. Wisdom and love grow together.

A famous zoology professor at the Sorbonne had the habit of giving his students an oral exam at the end of his course, and he always asked the same question: "Tell me all you know about worms."

Of course his students would goof around all semester and then just before the exam study assiduously all about worms. And they all got very high marks.

Finally the professor became concerned that all his students were doing so well. The time came to give the exam and meanwhile all the students were studying all about worms. When the first student came for the exam, the professor asked, "Tell me all you know about elephants."

The student was profoundly flustered for a moment, then he answered, "Elephants have worm-like tails. Worms are classified..." and then he started.

Knowledge is always unintelligent: if a question is asked for which you have a ready-made answer it is good; if a question is asked for which you don't have a ready-made answer you are in trouble. You are just behaving mechanically. Knowledge is mechanical, and how can anything mechanical help you to be wise? Knowledge is nothing but categorization.

Once upon a time there was a handsome young lion. He was captured in the African jungle and brought to America where he was put on display in a zoo. This made the lion very unhappy because he preferred the freedom of his wild native land and the companionship of other jungle beasts. But after a time he became resigned to his fate and made up his mind that if he had to live behind bars he would be the best zoo lion around.

In an adjoining cage there was another lion, an old and lazy one with a negative attitude and no signs of ambition or capability of any kind. He lay all day in the sun, aroused no interest from visitors. In sharp contrast, the young lion paced for hours back and forth in his cage. He acted the true King of Beasts, rolling his maned head, snarling and baring his teeth. The crowds loved him; they paid no attention to the indolent old lion asleep in the next cage.

The young lion appreciated the attention he was getting, but he was annoyed by his failure to win adequate reward. Each afternoon the zoo keeper came through the cages to feed the animals. The lazy old lion who made no effort to please the spectators was given a big bowl of red horse meat. The young lion, now a star attraction, was given a bowl of chopped-up oranges, bananas and nuts. This made him very unhappy.

"Perhaps," he mused, "I am not trying hard enough. I will improve the act." So he strutted longer and more spectacularly. To the snarls and gnashing of teeth he added frequent roars that shook the bars of his cage. The crowds got bigger. Thousands of citizens came to see his performance and he was pictured on page one in the local newspaper.

But the diet did not change. Still the lazy lion got the red meat and the young lion stayed on a vegetarian diet. Finally he could endure it no longer. He stopped the keeper with a challenge. "I am getting sick and tired of this," he complained. "Each day you give that no-good lazy type next door a big bowl of red meat and you feed me oranges, bananas and nuts. It is grossly unfair. Why do you think all these people come to the zoo? They come to see me! I am the star attraction, the lion that is doing all the work and the one that gets the results. Why am I not entitled to meat for dinner?"

The keeper replied, "Young man, you don't know how lucky you are. The Table of Organization in this zoo calls for one lion. You are being carried as a monkey!"

The philosophers are good at categorizing things; the scientists are good at categorizing things. Their whole effort is how to categorize, how to put everything in a particular category – this is this, that is that – and they go on and on. They are not in search of the organic unity of life, they are not in search of the ultimate principle of life that runs in the trees, and the mountains, and the stars, and the animals, and the birds, and men and women. They are not in search of that unifying factor. That unifying factor is what religions have called the truth, what Buddha has called nirvana, what Jesus has called the Kingdom of God.

You will not find any wisdom, any love in philosophy. Yes, you will find all kinds of beautiful answers; you will find all kinds of parrot-like information and facts. You will become very efficient in repeating them, in quoting them, but you will only be becoming a computer. That can be done better by a computer than by you.

Find out something within you which a computer cannot do and you will have found the right direction for your innermost being, for your freedom. That is the whole effort of Zen. That's what we are trying to do here. The computer cannot love; it can say, "I love you," but you know that it is a computer. It can make all the gestures of love, but if suddenly the electricity goes…"Grrr, grrr, grrr." Or if the battery runs out, you have to replace the battery, then it will say, "I love you."

But people are foolish and people are trying all kinds of things to make man more like a robot.

Just the other day I was reading this item in a newspaper, *Mundane Mating*, Toronto, 25th February:

"Men and women in the future will have robot sexual partners, and erotic technology will offer them their hearts' desires: stimulants, aphrodisiacs, and chemical orgasms.

"Sexologists concluded during a seminar here that men and women will still mate, but only during well-defined periods. Some said that women will want the 'profound and basic experience' of pregnancy without giving birth.

"One sexologist said that sexual relations with robots will help to 'supplement or enrich fantasy life and contribute to the establishment of a milieu which fosters rather than arrests sexual growth and development.'"

It is going to happen! In a way it has already happened. For thousands of years man has been making love mechanically, and the so-called mahatmas – Mahatma Gandhi and the Polack Pope and Mother Teresa – they all say that if you make love for one reason only – that is reproduction – then it is not sin. If you make love just for the sheer joy of it, for the sheer fun of it, it is sin.

Reproduction is chemical, biological; fun is a higher value. No animal knows anything about fun. Have you seen animals making love? Do you see any fun? They don't even say, "Hello!" to each other, and when they are finished they don't even say, "Thank you, see you soon!" They don't even look at each other; they seem to be utterly bored. Look at animals making love – they seem to be utterly bored, as if some biological force is forcing them to do something and they have to do it. Once they are finished they go on their ways; they will never recognize each other again, they will not write love letters.

Fun is not animal, fun is human. All these mahatmas go on condemning man for everything animal except reproduction – and reproduction is absolutely animal! All animals reproduce; there is nothing special in it. The only thing is they don't enjoy it, they don't have any fun in it, they don't have any loving relationship growing out of it, they don't transform the sexual energy. But reproduction is thought to be a virtue and fun is thought to be something absolutely condemnable. These people have always changed human joy into a robot-like phenomenon.

People have been making love to each other in the darkness, under blankets. If a Martian comes to the earth, particularly to India, he will not see any sign of anybody making love. He will be very puzzled about how these people reproduce. His basic inquiry here will be to find out how you reproduce, because he will not see any-body making love. Love is far away, he will not even see any people holding hands.

I have heard:

Once a couple reached Mars, and of course their basic inquiry was...because they could not find out how people made love there. They tried hard; they did all kinds of things that they had done on Earth to know about other people's love affairs – they became peeping toms – but they could not find out anything.

Finally they asked a Martian couple, very politely, "We have come from Earth, we are on a research tour. We want to know how you make love."

They said, "It is very simple!" They opened their fridge, brought out two jars, started mixing the chemicals in the jars into a third small jar, mixed them well and put the jars back into the fridge.

The couple inquiring about lovemaking could not see any love-making in it. They said, "What are you doing? Are you preparing coffee or something?"

The Martians said, "No, because in nine months this new jar will have a child in it. We have mixed all the ingredients needed. This is how we reproduce."

The couple from Earth started laughing. They said, "Then tell us one thing more – how do you prepare coffee?"

Then the Martians undressed and started making love! And the couple from Earth went into hysterical laughter; they could not believe what was happening. They were making coffee!

The Martians asked, "What are you laughing at? Why are you laughing?"

They said, "Because this is the way we reproduce – and you are making coffee! So this is the coffee which you served us this morning!"

Man has been trying to find some scientific way to reproduce so that everything can become mechanical. Then even love will no longer be private. Wisdom has already been taken over by the churches, the universities; love is still a little bit private. Of course, society has dominated almost ninety-nine percent of it through mar-riage, through all kinds of laws, through all kinds of legal bindings, but still one percent remains private. The society is not very happy about that part either; that part has also to be encroached upon – your love also has to be taken away from you. Wisdom was taken away long ago, now love has to be taken away. Then you are reduced to a machine, a servile machine, a slave; then you will only repeat cliches.

A man rings at the chaplain's door. When the housekeeper opens the door the man says, "I am bringing you the twenty-four thousand liters of oil you ordered."

The housekeeper is very surprised and asks the chaplain if he ordered all those liters of oil. The chaplain is even more surprised, but suddenly he remembers his parrot. So he storms into the room and shouts, "Did you order twenty-four thousand liters of oil?"

"No," says the parrot.

"Are you sure? Quite sure?" asks the chaplain.

"Yes!" shrills the parrot.

"Well, just wait!" replies the chaplain. "If I find out that you have been lying, I'll nail you by your two wings to the wall!"

Sure enough, he soon discovers that it is the parrot that placed the order, so he nails it to the wall.

After the parrot has been hanging there for a while, he sadly looks out of the window and sees the crucifix in front of the church. He lifts his head and says, "Well, Jesus, did you order twenty-four thousand liters of oil too?"

Man has been reduced to a parrot. My sannyasins have to come out of all these cages – the cages that philosophy, theology, science and all other kinds of things have created around you. You have to come out of it all, *in toto* – not partially, not gradually, not slowly, not tomorrow but now, at this very moment.

"Riko!"

"Yes, Master," said the official with a start.

"See," said Nansen, "the goose is out!"

Enough for today.

just see it

The first question:

Osho,
I feel that we need to hurry, that there is not much time left. The cocoon of slumber I am existing in seems to suffocate me, and I am afraid I will never make it.
You say the goose is out already. Why does it feel so impossible to grasp?

It is difficult to grasp because the goose *is* out; if it were in there would be no difficulty in grasping it. The bottle is dead, you can grasp it. The bottle is like a philosophy, theology, dogma, creed, cult, doctrine – just a corpse. The goose is alive, it is life itself; you cannot grasp it. It is not conceptual, it is existential. Who is going to grasp whom?

You are the goose! The mind is your bottle, and the mind is not something that can be broken. It is not material; it is just a thought, an imagination, the same stuff as dreams are made of. You cannot destroy a dream, you cannot kill a dream, you cannot cut a dream with a sword, you cannot burn it with fire. You just have to be awake, and the dream disappears. In fact, to say that the dream disappears is not right, because it was not there in the first place; it only appeared to be there.

That is the meaning of the Eastern word *maya*: illusion, a mirage – it appears but it exists not. You can see the horizon far away – it *appears;* it appears real. It seems that the earth is meeting the sky there; just a little effort and you will reach it. It seems within your capacity to reach it, but you can never reach it for the simple reason that it is only a mirage, it is not a reality. The earth and the sky never meet, there is no meeting place. So the closer you come to the so-called horizon, the more the horizon goes on and on disappearing ahead of you. The distance between you and the horizon always remains constant.

Albert Einstein says that the only thing constant in existence is the speed of light. I am not a physicist, I don't know whether he is right or wrong, but I know one thing which is absolutely constant and that is the distance between you and the horizon. That is absolutely constant – not a single inch less can it be, not a single inch more can it be. The difference, the distance, between the real and the unreal cannot be reduced.

The mind is unreal, hence it is not really a question of coming out of it; it is only a question of *seeing.*

Hence, the crazy master Nansen said, "See, the goose is out!" He was not making a logical statement – he was not saying, "See, *therefore* the goose is out." He was not even saying what Christmas Humphreys implies. Christmas Humphreys says, "There, the goose is out!" It cannot be said by Nansen. Nansen is not referring to there and here, he is not even referring to then and now. He is simply saying, "See, the goose is out! It has never been in, it cannot be in."

Your consciousness is always free, it is freedom itself. The problem is arising, because you want to grasp it. This is *mind* trying to grasp something which is beyond its capacities. The illusory cannot grasp the real and the real cannot grasp the illusory, remember. The illusory cannot grasp because it is not; the real cannot grasp the illusory because how can you grasp the illusory? It is not there at all.

Hence Gautama the Buddha says, "The moment you are absolutely empty and aware, all is found." It is only a question of shaking you up. It is a nightmare; the goose in the bottle is a nightmare. And sometimes it can happen in a very strange situation.

It happened in many strange situations in the past.

In Joseph Grimaldi's memoirs, as edited by Charles Dickens, there is the following story:

"In the July of this year a very extraordinary circumstance occurred at Sadler's Wells, which was the great topic of conversation in the neighborhood for some time afterward. It happened thus:

"Captain George Harris, of the Royal Navy, had recently returned to England after a long voyage. The crew had been paid off; many of them followed their commander to London and proceeded to enjoy themselves after the usual fashion of sailors. Sadler's Wells was at that time a famous place of resort with the blue jackets, the gallery being sometimes almost solely occupied by seamen and their female companions. A large body of Captain Harris' men resorted hither one night. Amongst them was a man who was deaf and dumb, and had been so for many years.

"This man was placed by his shipmates in the front row of the gallery. Grimaldi was in great form that night; although the audience was in one roar of laughter, nobody appeared to enjoy his fun and humor more than this poor fellow. His companions good-naturedly took a great deal of notice of him and one of them, who talked very well with his fingers, inquired how he liked the entertainments; to which the deaf-and-dumb man replied through the same medium, and with various gestures of great delight, that he had never seen anything half so comical before.

"As the scene progressed, Grimaldi's tricks and jokes became still more irresistible; and at length, after a violent peal of laughter and applause which quite shook the theater and in which the dumb man joined most heartily, he suddenly turned to his mate, who sat next to him, and cried out with much glee, 'What a damned funny fellow!' 'Why, Jack,' shouted the other man, starting back with great surprise, 'can you speak?' 'Speak!' replied the other, 'Ay, that I can, and hear, too.'

"Upon this the whole party, of course, gave three vehement cheers, and at the conclusion of the piece adjourned in a great procession with the recovered man, elevated on the shoulders of a half-dozen friends, in the center. A crowd of people quickly assembled round the door, and great excitement and curiosity were occasioned as the information ran from mouth to mouth that a deaf-and-dumb man had come to speak and hear, all owing to the cleverness of Joey Grimaldi.

"The landlady of the tavern, thinking Grimaldi would like to see his patient, told the man that if he would call next morning he would see the actor who had made him laugh so much. Grimaldi, being apprised of the circumstances, repaired to the house at the appointed time, and saw him, accompanied by several of his companions, all of whom still continued to manifest the liveliest interest in the sudden change that had happened to their friend, and kept on cheering and drinking and treating everybody in the house, in proof of their gratification.

"The man, who appeared an intelligent well-behaved fellow, said that in the early part of his life he could both speak and hear very well; and that he had attributed his deprivation of the two senses to the intense heat of the sun in the quarter of the world to which he had been and from which he had very recently returned. He added that on the previous evening he had for a long time felt a powerful anxiety to express his delight at what was passing on the stage; and that after some feat of Grimaldi's which struck him as being particularly amusing he had made a strong effort to deliver his thoughts, in which to his own astonishment, no less than that of his companions, he succeeded.

"Mr. Charles Dibdin, who was present, put several questions to the man; and from his answers it appeared to everyone present that he was speaking the truth. Indeed, his story was in some measure confirmed by Captain Harris himself; for one evening, about six months afterward, as Grimaldi was narrating the circumstances in the Green Room at Covent Garden, that gentleman, who chanced to be present, immediately remarked that he had no reason from the man's behavior while with him to suppose him an impostor, and that he had seen him on that day in full possession of his senses."

What actually happened? It was a laughter which shook him from his very roots. For a moment he forgot that he was in the bottle, for a moment he was outside the bottle, for a moment those forty years of deafness and dumbness disappeared. It is a simple forgetting.

That's what happens in the presence of a master. Sometimes it can happen without the master – Grimaldi was not Nansen. Grimaldi himself was surprised, he could not believe his eyes; he was not trying to wake the man up.

It has happened in the past in many strange situations, unexpectedly. In fact, it has happened more unexpectedly than it has ever happened with expectation, because expectation belongs to the mind, and when you are not expecting anything you are more relaxed, you are more calm, at ease. The goose can slip out of the nonexistential bottle more easily if it is relaxed. If it is tense and trying to get out of it, that very tension will keep it in.

That's what is happening to you. You say: "Why does it feel so impossible to grasp?"

It *is* impossible to grasp! If you are trying to grasp it, it is impossible; if you drop grasping, it is immediately possible, instantly possible – not even a single moment is lost.

The story is told that sometime in the last century a prominent European physician was examining an elderly man. After checking him over thoroughly and listening to his many vague complaints, the physician could find nothing physically wrong which would account for this patient's symptoms. We might imagine that it occurred to the doctor, just as it might to one of his latter-day colleagues, that his patient's physical complaints were in all probability serving as a mask for deep-seated emotional stress and depression.

Suddenly, an inspired idea came to him. He said to the old man that Joseph Grimaldi, perhaps the greatest clown of all times, was in town for a performance that very evening, and he told the whole story which I have just told you. The physician shrugged his shoulders about his inability to arrive at a diagnosis and suggested to the patient, "Why don't you go to see Grimaldi tonight?"

A distressed and disappointed expression suddenly played across the old man's face, and he exclaimed, "Oh, but you don't understand. I *am* Grimaldi!"

It has happened that in the company of a pseudo master somebody becomes enlightened; in a situation where no master was present, a natural accident took place, and somebody has become enlightened.

Lao Tzu became enlightened through seeing a dead leaf falling from a tree. He was sitting under a tree meditating for years, and nothing was happening – and he had been to great masters. Something was missing. He was trying too hard to grasp the truth; that very effort was the barrier. That early spring morning, the birds singing, the trees swaying, the sun shining, the fragrance of the flowers… He forgot all about enlightenment.

Once in a while it is very good to forget all about enlightenment; otherwise it can drive you nuts – more than anything else! Money will not drive you as crazy, nor will politics, because they are all graspable. If you try hard you can get as much money as you want; just a little effort, a little cunningness, a little calculation – something Jewish in your blood – and you can manage. Something of the insane in you, and you can become a politician.

When Adolf Hitler started, nobody ever thought that he would become one of the greatest historical figures of the twentieth century. Two friends, a great psychologist and a great theologian, heard him speak for the first time, and both agreed that this insane man would never be able to make his name in any possible way. Both agreed on it: one was an expert in psychological matters; the other was an expert in theological matters. It was a great agreement between a psychologist and a spiritualist.

The man who was a theologian finally became the Pope. By that time Adolf Hitler had become the most powerful man in the world. The Pope's old psychologist friend came to see him and he reminded him, "What do you say about it now? We both agreed that this man would never make his name in the world of politics; he was simply insane. Who was going to be impressed by him in a country like Germany which can brag about its intelligence and brag sincerely, truthfully? It is one of the most intelligent countries in the world. Who was going to be befooled by this maniac? We agreed, but what do you say now? He has made his mark; his name is going to remain part of history forever."

The Pope looked at the psychologist and said, "Yes, I made that comment, but at that time I was not infallible!"

Neurotics, nuts, cuckoos, they can make their name, they can be great politicians, they can be the wealthiest people in the world, they can become very famous. All that is needed is a crazy urge to be on top – it is graspable.

Enlightenment is ungraspable, so the more you try to grasp it, the less it is possible. You cannot hold enlightenment in your fist – the tighter the fist, the less is the possibility. But you can hold enlightenment in your open hands; that is the only way to hold it. In your open hands you can hold the whole sky, all the stars, the whole existence, but in your closed fist there is nothing. The more closed it is, the more tight it is, the less is the possibility of anything being there. Enlightenment has to be achieved with open hands, by a relaxed, calm, quiet resting in your being.

It happened to Lao Tzu that way. For years he was trying to grasp and grasp, and nothing was happening. That morning he simply forgot all about it. It was so beautiful, so sunny, there was so much delight all around, who cared about enlightenment? For a moment that ambition was put aside. And just by coincidence a dead leaf, which must have been hanging off the tree, started falling.

Lao Tzu saw it falling from above, slowly, slowly. He watched it, he became just a watcher; there was nothing to do. He observed it: he remained aware of the swaying, and the leaf falling in the subtle breeze of the morning. As it settled on the ground something settled in Lao Tzu too. Suddenly the feeling of "Eureka!" Suddenly a great outburst of joy: "Aha!" He danced…the goose was out!

When the goose is out, what else can you do except dance, sing, laugh – laugh at the whole absurdity of it all, that you were never in, though you had believed that you were in? Your belief was the only imprisonment.

You ask me: "I feel that we need to hurry…"

What is the hurry? All of eternity is yours! You have always been here, you *are* here, you will *always* be here. Nothing is ever lost. Now it is a confirmed scientific truth that nothing is ever destroyed. If matter is not destroyed, why should consciousness be destroyed? Matter belongs to a very gross plane of existence. If the gross plane is so valued by existence, do you think the higher manifestation is not valued by existence? The higher plane is *more* valued! If matter persists and is impossible to destroy, consciousness cannot be destroyed either. It is the highest expression of life; there is nothing higher. It is the very Everest of life, the peak beyond which there is nothing. All of existence is moving toward that peak. There is no hurry.

The whole idea of hurry is a creation of the mind. Let me say it in this way: mind and time are synonymous; the moment your mind stops, time also stops. The more you are in your mind, the more you are in time; the less you are in your mind, the more you are out of time.

There is a famous statement of Jesus Christ – of course, this is not related in the Bible. The Bible has missed many beautiful statements of Jesus, but truth has its own way of persisting. It has been carried by the Sufi mystics down through the ages.

The statement is: somebody asked Jesus, "You talk again and again about the Kingdom of God. What will be the most special thing about the Kingdom of God? What will be the most unique phenomenon in this Kingdom of God that you talk about?"

Jesus said – it is a very simple statement but very pregnant; he said, "There shall be time no longer." Strange, unexpected. One would have expected something else from Jesus: God the Father will be there; the Holy Ghost will be there; all the saints will be there, and angels will be playing "alleluia" on their harps – something like that. And what he said was totally different. He said, "There shall be time no longer" – and he was right.

Eternity means timelessness. But the Judaic tradition out of which three religions were born – the Jewish religion, the Christian religion and the Mohammedan religion –all contain the idea of one life. That idea of one life creates hurry, worry, a constant rush to reach, not knowing exactly where you want to reach to, or what to reach for, or what you will do even if you do reach the goal. A craziness has been created because time is short, and it is slipping out of your hands, and soon death will knock on the doors, and you are still unfulfilled – nothing special has happened yet.

Hence, as days pass your anguish becomes deeper and deeper; your anxiety becomes greater and greater. Your life becomes a burden; you start dragging yourself. You are constantly trembling and afraid that you are not going to make it.

That's what is in this question. It reads: "The cocoon of slumber I am existing in seems to suffocate me, and I am afraid I will never make it."

There is nothing to make! All that is needed has happened; it is there from the very beginning. You have to enjoy it, not make it. You have to rejoice in it, not make it. The idea of a small span of life, say seventy years, gives rise to a great trembling, because one-third of it will be lost in sleep, another third will be lost in education, schools, colleges, universities and all kinds of nonsense. The remaining third will be wasted in earning bread and butter, quarreling with the wife, taking care of the children, nagging the husband, fighting with the neighbors, competing for this and that.

In fact, if you sit down quietly one day and write down how your life has been spent up to now, you will be shocked! What have you been doing? Even small things take much of your time – shaving your beard and mustache every day... Look at women standing before the mirror for hours – even the mirrors get tired! How much time are you wasting reading the same stupid newspapers every day? It is the same story –nothing new ever happens. There is no news, it is all old – the same rape that has been happening for thousands of years...

Just the other day Sheela brought me a cutting from an English newspaper. A bishop – and who else? – had been sentenced to twelve years' jail time for raping many women. That was his only work; he was doing it religiously. But this is not an exception; the poor bishop's only fault was that he was caught; otherwise all bishops are bound to do it. They are ordained to do it, disciplined to do it! Their whole lives are structured such that they have to be phony, pseudo, double. He was living a double life, and all the rapes that he committed were committed after his beautiful, spiritual sermons. First he would sermonize about the great things of life – and celibacy must have been one of those great things – and then, because of his beautiful sermons, his learned scholarship and his mask of a religious holy man, he was able to seduce all kinds of women. And they were innocent girls, fourteen, sixteen, eighteen years old. He had been doing it for years, but when you do it behind a religious screen it is easier.

It was a long report, a full-page story: I told Sheela, "Keep it, because this is an old thing; it has always been happening. This is what the *rishis*, the *munis*, the bishops, the saints have always been doing. This man is unfortunate."

One of my teachers, a very beautiful old man, used to say before every examination in school... He used to be the superintendent of the examinations. I loved that old man, his honesty, his truthfulness. He would come and tell all the students, "I am not against it if you are copying from others, or if you have brought books with you, or if you have brought notes with you – that has nothing to do with me. My whole concern is that you should not be caught. If you are caught then you will be in difficulty, so make sure... If you are certain you will not be caught there will be no problem with me, but if you are caught then I cannot save you."

So he would say, "I will give you five minutes. Close your eyes and ponder over the situation, and those who have brought books, notes, etcetera, to cheat with can give them to me – no notice will be taken. But once you decide to cheat then don't get caught. Then be clever enough; then be intelligent enough... And remember one thing: that if you are intelligent enough you need not have those notes! So let me warn you that having those notes simply proves you are not intelligent enough, and you will be caught!"

Immediately people would start bringing their copies, their notes, and he would gather them from almost everybody!

I loved that old man, he was sincere. He was saying that the question is not that you are cheating, the question is that you should not be caught.

What you read in the newspapers is that some people have been caught. Everybody is doing the same – with very few differences. The quantity may be different but the quality is the same. Murders are being done, rapes are being done, wars continue, all kinds of stupid things go on and on for centuries, and you are reading all these things and wasting your time, seeing a movie, seeing a TV show or listening to the same old scriptures. You have heard them thousands of times, you know the whole story, but still you go on keeping yourself occupied.

If in a seventy-year life you can find even seven minutes which were just yours – unoccupied, undistracted, relaxed, resting in your own being – that will be enough. But those seven minutes are missing, hence the hurry. Life is short and it is running by, and there is no other life. Death will come and you will die utterly empty, unfulfilled. This hurry is not going to help, this hurry simply makes things more difficult. It keeps you running, certainly, it keeps you chasing shadows, but while you are chasing shadows you are again wasting your time.

So, you say: "I feel that we need to hurry..."

If you are here with me forget all about hurrying, forget all about time. Jesus says: "There shall be time no longer in my Kingdom of God." I say to you: drop time, and this very moment, here and now, you are in the Kingdom of God. Why wait for the Kingdom of God? I would like to reverse Jesus's statement. He says: "Enter the Kingdom of God, because there shall be time no longer". This is not right; it is putting the horse behind the cart. How will you enter the Kingdom of God? Where will you enter the Kingdom of God from? The very idea that there will no longer be any time in the Kingdom of God will put you in a deep hurry: "How to reach it quickly? How to enter the Kingdom of God so that there will be no time, no problem, no anxiety, and one will live in the eternal now?" But that "now" becomes a "then." *Now* becomes a goal.

If you see the point, I say drop time, and in that very dropping the goose is out – because time is mind. Drop time and you *are* in the Kingdom of God. Not only are you in the Kingdom of God, but you have always been in it – time was creating a nightmare around you, your mind was there fabricating all kinds of dreams. You were surrounded by a mist of your own creation.

You say: "The cocoon of slumber I am existing in seems to suffocate me, and I am afraid I will never make it."

I am also afraid! If you try to make it, you will never make it. Drop the whole idea of making it, forget all about it. Rejoice in the moment! Can't you listen to the distant call of the cuckoo, can't you listen to the crows, can't you listen to the birds? They are now and here. No hurry, no yesterdays, no tomorrows.

Jesus says to his disciples, "Look at the beautiful lilies in the field. They are far more beautiful; they have far more grandeur than even King Solomon had, attired in all his glory." What is the secret of those poor lilies? The secret, Jesus says, is that they think not of the morrow, they live now. Life is now, so there is no need to make it. It is already here! You are in it!

Kabir says; "You are like a fish which is thirsty in the ocean." You are born in it, you are part of it, you live in it, you are a manifestation of it and you will disappear into it. You are just like a wave in the ocean. But the fish is thirsty in the ocean because she is contemplating some other ocean, some other life, some other time, some other space, some Kingdom of God.

Drop all that rubbish! There is no other Kingdom of God than this moment. The trees are already in it, the mountains are already in it, the stars are already in it – only man has fallen away, only man has gone astray. The reason why man has gone astray is his effort to grasp it, to understand it, to make a conceptual system in which he can logically put everything. Existence is paradoxical. If you try to make it logical you are never going to make it, you are never going to grasp it.

You say: "Osho, you say the goose is out already. Why does it feel so impossible to grasp?"

Because it is already out! Just see the point; don't think about it.

A moment's thought and you have gone far away. Don't brood about it, just see it. It is not a question of thinking about and about, going in circles, it is not a question of great intellectuality, of philosophical acumen, of logical efficiency. It is not a question of a trained mind, it is a question of an innocent heart.

Just see it! Wipe your eyes of all the tears, wipe your eyes of all the dust that has accumulated on them, and just look at existence. A leaf falling from the tree may become your enlightenment.

Buddha became enlightened seeing the last star in the morning disappearing. As the star disappeared, Buddha became enlightened.

Enlightenment is not something that has to be achieved, it is something that is your very nature. So don't try to chase your own tail. You must have seen dogs doing it... Dogs are very philosophical, Aristotelian; they suffer from aristotolitis! You can see them in the winter morning enjoying the sun, but they cannot fully enjoy it because of the tail. The tail is always there; they would like to catch hold of it. They jump, and the tail jumps away, they jump harder – a logical conclusion: you have not jumped hard enough, you have to make a greater effort. The greater the effort they make, the faster the tail jumps – and they start going crazy. It is the dog's own tail; there is no need to chase it.

Existence, enlightenment, truth, they all belong to you; there is no need to grasp, to achieve in the first place. And *then* it is achieved, and *then* it is grasped.

The second question:

Osho,
I am a radical revolutionary politician. Have you something to say to me?

You have already gone too far, you will not listen. Just to be a politician is enough, but you are a revolutionary radical politician – cancer doubled, trebled! Is not politics enough? Do you also have to be radical, revolutionary? We always find beautiful words to hide ugly realities.

No politician can be revolutionary, because the only revolution is spiritual. No politician can be radical either; the very word *radical* means concerning the roots. The politician only prunes the leaves;

he has nothing to do with the roots. Only enlightenment takes you to the roots, only meditation takes you to the roots of the problems.

Politics has always existed, politicians have always existed, but what has happened? The world remains the same sorry-go-round! In fact, misery goes on becoming multiplied every day. All these revolutionaries and radical politicians have only proved to be mischievous – with good intentions, of course. But intentions don't count at all; what counts is consciousness.

The politician has no consciousness; in fact, he is trying to avoid his own inner problems, he is trying to escape from his own problems. The easiest way to escape from oneself is to become concerned about world problems, economics, politics, history, service to the poor, transformation of the conditions of society, reformation. All these are strategies for escaping from one's own problems, subtle strategies – dangerous, because one feels that one is doing something great, while one is simply being a coward.

First face *your* own problems, encounter them. First try to transform your being. Only a transformed person can trigger processes of transformation in others.

You ask me: "Have you something to say to me?"

Remember two things. First, the three rules of ruination. There are three ways to be ruined in this world: first is by sex, second is by gambling, and the third is by politics. Sex is the most fun; gambling is the most exciting; and politics is the surest.

The second rule, remember the fundamental law of all revolutions: when the revolution comes, things will be different – not better, just different.

Politicians have been driving the whole world for centuries – where to, to what end? Is it not time that we see the stupidity of the whole game? At least we are aware, fully aware, of five thousand years of politics; before that the case must have been the same. But in five thousand years of political games what has happened? Man remains in the same darkness, in the same misery, in the same hell. Yes, politics goes on giving man hope, a hope for a better tomorrow which never comes. Tomorrows never come.

It is the opiate of the people. Karl Marx says religion is the opiate of the people. It is true, it is true ninety-nine point nine percent; only point one percent it is not true. A Buddha, a Jesus, a Lao Tzu, a Zarathustra, these few people can be counted in that point one percent. Otherwise Karl Marx is ninety-nine point nine percent accurate; religion has proved the opiate of the people. It has kept people in a drugged state, in such a sleep that they can tolerate an intolerable existence – they can tolerate all kinds of slavery, starvation – in the hope of a better tomorrow. Religions used to provide a better tomorrow in the other world, after death.

People come to me and ask, "What will happen after death?" I don't answer them; I ask them another question instead. I ask them, "Forget all about after death, let me ask you one thing: "What is happening before death?" Because whatsoever is happening before death will continue to happen after death. It is a continuum: your consciousness will be the same – before or after will not make any difference. The body may not be the same, the container may change, but the content will remain the same. Whatsoever happens is happening to the content, not to the container.

Think about the goose, don't be bothered about the bottle. You may have a different bottle, better produced, of better material, more sophisticated, a crystal bottle, a diamond bottle, but that does not make any difference. What makes the difference is your consciousness – the goose.

First, religion was giving opiate to the people *tomorrow, after death*. Millions of people remained in that state of druggedness, under that chloroform – religious chloroform. Now politics is doing the same. Even communism has proved nothing but a new opiate for the masses – communism is a new kind of religion. The strategy is the same: "Tomorrow will come the revolution, and everything will be all right." You have to sacrifice your today for tomorrow, and tomorrow never comes.

Sixty years have passed since the Russian revolution, and tomorrow is still as far away as before. Thirty years have passed since the Indian revolution, the Gandhian revolution, and tomorrow remains as far away, in fact, farther away than before. The people who sacrificed sacrificed in vain; it would have been better if they had lived. The people who were killed were really committing suicide, hoping that they were doing a great service to humanity.

Don't create more madness in the world; it is already full of madness.

A colleague of mine once worked in a mental hospital. While

making the rounds he would test the patient by asking, "Why are you here?" The response usually revealed the patient's degree of reality orientation.

One morning the psychologist received a response that rocked him. "I am here," replied the patient, "for the same reason you are, doctor: I couldn't make a go of it in the outside world."

The patients and the doctors, the people and the politicians are all in the same boat. They are all Ayatollah Khomaniacs! All kinds of maniacs are loose in the world. If you drop out of your radical revolutionary politics there will be at least one Khomaniac less, and that will be a great blessing.

The third question:

Osho,
I have heard you say that knowledge is useless. Then what is needed to guide us to the ultimate goal?

There is one good thing about your question that I appreciate: you say, "I have heard you say." All the Buddhist scriptures begin in that way; that is a very sincere thing. The Christian, the Judaic, the Hindu, the Mohammedan scriptures don't begin that way, but all Buddhist scriptures begin, "I have heard the master say" – because it is not a question whether the master has said it or not, "I have heard it"; these are two different things. The master may have said one thing; you may have heard something totally different, because between you and the master there is a great barrier – the barrier of the mind – prejudices, concepts, preconceived ideas. So what you hear is not necessarily the thing that is said.

This is good that you say, "I have heard you say." You are not saying that I have said it. You are saying, "I have heard…" It may be right, it may not be right; I may have said it, I may not have said it.

This has to be remembered by all of my sannyasins: whenever you are quoting me, remember, it is what you have heard. There is a possibility it may have been said, there is a possibility it may not have been said at all; something else may have been said.

And that's actually what has happened.

You say: "I have heard you say that knowledge is useless."

No, I have not said that. Knowledge is very useful – wisdom is useless! Knowledge is needed in the marketplace, in business, in politics. Everywhere knowledge is needed – in technology, in science – everywhere knowledge is needed. Knowledge is very useful, utilitarian. Wisdom is absolutely useless, but that's its beauty. It is not a commodity, you cannot use it in any way; you cannot sell it, you cannot purchase it. It does not belong to the utilitarian world; it is a flowering.

What use is a rose flower? What use is the song of a bird? What use is it? If you look around in existence – the stars, the clouds, the mountains, the rivers – what is the use of it all? It is all useless. Why are butterflies so beautiful? Why does God take so much care in painting their wings? What is the point of it all?

Remember, the outside world is the world of utility; the inside world is the world of significance, not of utility. The outside world has a totally different dimension – it is needed. You need bread, you need butter, you need a house, you need medicine, you need clothes, shelter; you need thousands of things. But the inner world is simply one of luxury; it is not a need, it is a joy. It is sheer rejoicing.

If somebody asks you, "What is the use of love?" the question is unanswerable, by the very use of the word *use*. Love is not a commodity, the world can go on without love – it is already going on without it. Everything is going perfectly well; in fact, it is only when love happens that some disturbance happens. Hence, all societies are against love.

The world will go on perfectly well without musicians. Who needs musicians? They will not be able to drive a train, to pilot an airplane; they are not reliable people.

I used to travel in India. One of my friends who died just a few months ago was a lover of traveling. I used to go on the fastest trains possible, because I had to cover the whole country. He loved to travel by passenger trains which stopped at every station, every small station. The journey that could have been completed within ten hours would take four days, five days, sometimes seven days. Whenever he was with me he would insist.

One time I agreed and it was really a joy, because he knew every place where the tea was the best, where the milk was the purest, where you could get a good sweet, where you could get good apples, mangoes. In those five days of traveling with him I forgot all about where we were going – there was no need to go anywhere! And everybody knew him – the porters, the stationmasters, the drivers – because he was always traveling on these slow trains. At each station the train would stop for one hour, half an hour, two hours.

One small station was a really beautiful place. The whole station was surrounded by a big mango grove, hundreds of mango trees. He took me out of the station and he started climbing a tree. I said, "What are you doing?" He said, "The mangoes are ripe!" And I said, "If the train leaves we will be in difficulty!" He said, "Don't be worried. Come along with me." I went with him. I was constantly telling him, "It is time now, the train will leave." He said, "Don't be worried. Do you see the man above us?" There was one man up in the tree. He said, "He is the driver. Unless he gets down, the train cannot move!"

I enjoyed that moment!

Life can be lived either with utility as your very style or it can be lived as a playfulness. Music, love, flowers, stars, poetry, painting, dancing, all belongs to the inner world. I am not against knowledge; when you are doing something in the world use your knowledge. There, to use wisdom is foolish; there, sitting in a car and meditating is dangerous. There, you should use all of your efficiency, all of your knowledge, all of your know-how, but you should not be confined by it. You should not become obsessed with it; you should be able to go inside. When the work is over you should be able to close the doors to the outside world and return to the inner. Then dance, sing, meditate, love, live. One should be flexible, liquid.

This misunderstanding is possible with me, but you can see my approach if you don't bring your mind in. I am not telling you to renounce the world for the simple reason that you can always use your knowledge. Sitting in a cave in the Himalayas you will not be able to use your knowledge. The outside world is as beautiful as the inside world: if we can have both, why choose one?

My whole message is that you can eat the cake and have it too, so why go for half? Knowledge is useful in the outside world, in the inside world it is a hindrance. The same is true about the inner wisdom: it is of immense joy inside, but don't try to use it outside.

Both things have been done. The West has lived through knowledge only; hence it has lost the inner dimension. It has lost the inner flowering, and it has lost contact with its own being. The East has done the reverse: thinking that knowledge is useless, it has become unscientific, non-utilitarian, so its outside world has become shrunken. It is poor, ugly, unscientific.

The West has lost contact with its own soul, and the East has lost contact with its own body. Man is a dance of these two complements; these two are partners in the dance. These two are like two wings: you cannot fly into the sky with only one wing. With one wing, you will fall. The West has fallen, the East has fallen; both have proved to be utter failures.

We need a new kind of human being who has both wings: the wing of knowledge – science, technology – and the wing of meditation – enlightenment, love, and freedom. When both wings are functioning in a deep synchronicity, in a deep togetherness, in accord and harmony, only then is man complete, total.

Knowledge is not needed for the inner world. About the inner world, you ask: "Then what is needed to guide us to the ultimate goal?"

There is no ultimate goal – let it be clear from the very beginning. There is no goal as such; hence there is no question of there being an ultimate goal. All that is, is immediate – let me repeat, *immediate*. There is nothing ultimate anywhere; immediacy itself is the ultimate. There is no goal; the pilgrimage itself is the goal. Each step is the goal, each moment is the goal.

For that, knowledge is not needed because knowledge is a guide for goals, for achievements. For that goal-less, immediate life, innocence is needed, not knowledge. Innocence, like a child – what Dionysus calls a "luminous ignorance" –that is exactly what is needed; a luminous ignorance, an enlightened state of not-knowing.

You always think in terms of enlightenment, as if it were the ultimate in knowing. You are wrong. Enlightenment is the ultimate state of not-knowing; it is luminous ignorance, it is child-like. The sage again becomes a child. He starts collecting on the beach – colored stones, pebbles, seashells. He starts collecting wildflowers for no reason at all, just for the sheer joy of it.

The Sunday school teacher asked her class of youngsters if they could name any of the Ten Commandments, and the kindergarten-aged boy stood up and announced proudly, "Thou shalt not omit adultery!"

This is luminous ignorance, so innocent: "Thou shalt not omit adultery!"

The pretty young schoolteacher was concerned about one of her eleven-year-old students. Taking him aside after class one day, she asked, "Victor, why has your schoolwork been so poor lately?"

"I can't concentrate," replied the lad. "I'm afraid I have fallen in love."

"Is that so?" said the teacher, holding back an urge to smile. "And with whom?"

"With you," he answered.

"But Victor," exclaimed the secretly pleased young lady, "don't you see how silly that is? It's true that I would like a husband of my own someday, but I don't want a child."

"Oh, don't worry," said Victor reassuringly, "I'll be careful!"

A stern father was taking his little son Johnny for a walk in the park when suddenly a honeybee settled on a rock in front of them. Just for spite, the boy smashed it with a rock, whereupon his father said, "That was cruel, and for being cruel you'll get no honey for a whole year."

Later, Johnny deliberately stepped on a butterfly. "And for that, young man," said the father, "you will get no butter for a year." When they returned home, Johnny's mother was busy fixing dinner. Just as they entered the kitchen, she spied a cockroach and immediately crushed it. The little boy looked at his father impishly and said, "Shall I tell her, dad, or will you?"

The grade school principal dropped into the new third-grade teacher's room to see how she was adjusting to her first day of school. "There is one problem," she said. "That little boy in the first row belongs in the second grade but insists on remaining here, and he is so smart I hate to send him back."

"He can't be that smart," said the principal. "Ask him something."

The teacher called the boy forward and inquired, "What does a dog do on three legs that a man does on two legs that I do sitting down?"

"Shake hands," said the boy.

"What has a cow got four of that I have only two of?" she went on.

"Legs," the boy replied.

"What is a four-letter word meaning intercourse?" she continued.

"Talk," he answered.

The teacher turned to the principal. "Well, what should I do?"

He drew her aside and whispered, "Better promote him to the fourth grade. I missed all three questions!"

The fourth question:

Osho,
Will you say something serious so that I can also understand?

This is really a difficult question! I don't know what seriousness is. I can try, but I don't think I will succeed. I have never been serious – the more serious I look, the less I am! But let us try a few things for you. Who knows? You may get something serious out of it. People get all kinds of things which I have not said, which I have not meant, which I have not even dreamed of. And you may even understand something!

In the old days it was the custom in the old Jewish villages that the night after someone got married the rabbi would come and inspect the bedsheets to see that the bride had been a virgin.

The young bride knew this and also knew she would not pass the test. So she got up in the middle of the night and put some spots of ink on the bedsheet, but as it was dark she grabbed the wrong bottle and got green ink.

The next morning, the rabbi came as expected and did his inspection. Suddenly he shouted, "What a monster! He poked her through the gallbladder!"

No, it was not serious! Let us try again.

An old gentleman and an old lady have a conversation. They talk about the good old times and he asks her, "Excuse me, did you ever blush?"

"Oh yes," she says, "four times. The first time when I undressed in front of my husband. The second time when I undressed in front of my lover. The third time when I took money for it. And the fourth time when I paid someone for it. And you?"

The man is silent for a moment and then says, "I blushed twice. The first time when I couldn't do it the second time. And the second time when I couldn't do it the first time."

I missed again! I am not a good archer, because I don't believe in targets and goals, so my arrows go everywhere except the target.
The last attempt:

It is the annual hunting season in heaven. But the Holy Ghost is reluctant to participate – every year up to now he has ended up with a shot in his bum.

God the Father finally convinces him to participate and promises to watch over him carefully. But toward the end it happens again: there is a shot and the Holy Ghost jumps around in agony, hands on his lower back.

In rage, God the Father runs into the bushes and pulls Joseph out. "Joseph!" he screams. "Will you never be able to forgive what he did with Mary?"

Enough for today.

no peaks, no valleys

The first question:

Osho,
You are calling from the peak. I am lost in the echoing valleys.
How may I come to you?

There are no peaks, no valleys; the whole idea is a fabricated. There is no higher, no lower; there is no hierarchy in existence at all. It is just one cosmic whole; it is an organic unity.

The egoist has always been trying to divide people into different categories: the ignorant, the enlightened; the sinners, the saints; the criminals, the virtuous; the notorious, the famous; the moral, the immoral. The game is the same: divide people and then try to belong to the higher category so you can pretend to be "holier than thou."

Hence, I want it to be continuously remembered by you that there are no peaks, and there are no valleys; we all belong to one oceanic whole. The smallest blade of grass is as significant as the greatest star. They all participate in the same cosmic play; they all contribute to its beauty, to its joy, to its song, to its celebration. Existence will be less even if a small blade of grass is missing; there will be something lacking, there will be an emptiness.

My approach to life is non-divisive. My sannyasins are not my followers; they are not to imitate me; they are not to become me. So, don't use such language; don't use such concepts. Don't say: "Osho, you are calling from the peak. I am lost in the echoing valleys."

The peaks and the valleys are part of one whole: the peaks cannot exist without the valleys; the valleys cannot exist without the peaks. So which is important? Both are interdependent. Life is neither dependent nor independent; life is a continuum of interdependence. It is beautiful wherever you are; it is lovely to be whatsoever you are.

The desire to be on the peaks is a wrong desire. All desires as such are wrong, and religious desires are far worse than any other desires for the simple reason that other desires can be fulfilled. Of course, even by their fulfillment you will not go beyond frustration; fulfilled or not fulfilled, frustration is inevitable. If your desire is fulfilled you will be frustrated –because now you will see you were chasing a shadow; you have got it and there is nothing in it. If your desire is not fulfilled you will be frustrated, because your whole life is wasted and you have not been able to fulfill a single desire. All your hopes are shattered.

Hopes are bound to be shattered. To hope is to hanker for hopelessness, to desire is to breed frustration. In worldly things at least there is a possibility of succeeding, failing, attaining, not attaining. But in spiritual matters there is no question of attainment at all because the goose is out! Nothing can be done about it; it is already out. The moment you start enjoying your valley you are on the peak – there is no other peak!

One day I suddenly decided, enough is enough. I dropped the idea of the peaks and started enjoying the valley, and I saw a miracle: the valley disappeared. In fact, from the very beginning there had been no valley, I was always on the peak – but because I was searching for a peak I could not see where I was.

Your eyes are focused far away, hence you miss the obvious. It is here, and your mind is there, arrowed into the blue sky. The reality surrounds you: it is closer than your very heartbeat, it is closer than your breathing, it is closer than the circulation of your blood, it is closer than your very marrow, it is closer than your very consciousness. It is your very core, your very being!

Don't ask for the peak, otherwise you will go on missing it.

The more you miss the more you will be in a vicious circle, because the more you miss the more you try to reach. The more you miss the greater the endeavor, the more you miss the more you become an American: "Try it again and again, try harder." A simple conclusion: if you are missing, that shows you are not trying hard enough, so put your total energy into it. And you will *still* be missing; there is no way to make it. You are trying for the impossible and the impossible does not happen; it cannot happen, it has never happened – it is not in the nature of things.

Buddha said again and again, "*Aes dhammo sanantano*": this *is* the nature of things. Listen to the nature of things and you will never be in misery; try to improve upon it and you will live in hell. Hell is our creation, and we create hell by trying to do the impossible. Heaven is our nature, it is our spontaneity, it is where we always are.

You have heard the biblical story that God threw Adam and Eve out of his kingdom, the Garden of Eden. It is basically wrong; it is wrong for two reasons. First: the reason why he threw them out is very despotic – they had not obeyed him. He seems to be a very ordinary daddy, too ordinary, fanatic! A small, childish rebellion, which is part of nature, part of growth… We should be immensely grateful to Adam and Eve because they disobeyed. That is the beginning of humanity, that is the beginning of revolution, that is the beginning of growth, of maturity, of freedom, of a sense of dignity. They revolted against being animals. All other animals were very good Catholics, all going to church every Sunday, reading the Bible, following the command- ments, following every order without ever questioning it. They are still doing the same, hence dogs have remained dogs, eagles have remained eagles, buffaloes have remained buffaloes, donkeys, howso- ever saintly and holy they look, have remained donkeys. Only man has grown; his growth started with the rebellion.

The rebellion was simple – every child has to go through it. A moment comes when the child has to say no, he has to insist on the no. In fact, unless a child learns to say no he will never be able to say yes; his yes will be impotent without a background of no. A funda- mental no is needed as a blackboard; only on that fundamental blackboard of no can he write a beautiful yes.

God denied man his fundamental right to say no, and in that very denial he denied man's ultimate growth to say yes. The whole story is fanatical, ugly.

Second: where can you drive man out to? All of existence is the Garden of Eden! There is no other place, there is no other space, there is no other time. The whole universe is divine, so wherever you are you are in the Garden of Eden. The idea has been implanted in man that you have to reach the Garden of Eden. You are in the garden, and the idea that you have been thrown out of the garden and that you have to get back to the garden is creating your whole trouble, your whole misery, your whole anguish. Not recognizing where you are, you are hankering for something which is not possible, because this *is* the place. "This very body the buddha; *this very place* the lotus paradise." There is no other buddhahood, and there is no other lotus paradise.

The word *paradise* comes from the Persian *firdaus*; *firdaus* means a garden – the same story, the Garden of Eden. Everybody is searching for a paradise. You can give it different names – nirvana, enlightenment, *samadhi*, Kingdom of God, ultimate truth – you can go on giving it different names. But you will still be missing – missing not because you have been thrown out of the garden, but missing because you are in the garden and you have fallen into a deep dream-like state. The dream consists of your desires to reach somewhere else, to reach to the peaks.

My insistence is that you are already there. Just sit silently and look around; sit silently and look within. You have never been anywhere else! *Aes Dhammo Sanantano* – this *is* the nature of things – you cannot be anywhere else.

A rose is a rose is a rose, there is no other possibility. But you can drive a rose crazy – you can put the idea into the mind of the rose that "You have to be a rose. What are you doing here? Wasting time, wasting a great opportunity. God has given you an opportunity to be a rose. What are you doing here? Swaying in the wind, dancing in the sun, taking life as fun? Be serious, be somber, become holy! Read the Koran, the Gita, the Bible," and you will have driven the rose crazy.

It is good that roses don't understand your language. It is good that they don't care a bit about what you are saying. It is good that they go on doing their thing without bothering at all about your politicians, your priests, your professors. That's why they are so beautiful, so innocent. Your priests cannot be so beautiful, they cannot be so innocent; they are bound to be cunning.

After checking into the large motel complex, the evangelist read in his room for several hours, then sauntered over to the bar where he struck up a conversation with the pretty hat check girl. After she had finished working they shared a few drinks and then retired to his room. But when the evangelist began removing her blouse she seemed to have second thoughts. "Are you sure this is alright?" she asked. "I mean, you are a holy man."

"My dear," he replied, "it is written in the Bible."

She took him at his word, and the two spent a very pleasant night together. The next morning, however, as the girl was preparing to leave, she said, "You know, I don't remember the part of the Bible you mentioned last night. Could you show it to me?"

In response, the evangelist took the Gideon Bible from the nightstand, opened the cover and pointed to the flyleaf on which someone had inscribed, "The hat check girl screws."

These are your priests, your evangelists, your great spiritual leaders! They are neurotic and they are driving the whole of humanity neurotic. Avoid all spiritual nonsense – and spiritual nonsense is *real* nonsense; all other nonsense is very ordinary, very mundane. In fact, with mundane matters you cannot be too nonsensical – reality will prevent it, science will prevent it, your own sense of pragmatism will prevent it. But with religious nonsense there are no checks. There is no reality, no criterion so that you can judge, so you can fly off into all kinds of esoteric bullshit.

Your priests are such bullshitters; for centuries they have been bullshitting you! You are crawling in holy cowdung! It is time to get out of it.

The way you are is the only way you can be. Accept it – not only accept it but rejoice in it, love it, and the peak will start opening up within your very heart. Suddenly you will find you are awake in the Garden of Eden, immediately. It is not a question of going anywhere, just of being here.

You ask me: "How may I come to you?"

There is no need. You have to come to *you*, not to me. I am not here to create a new kind of neurosis. There are enough alternatives available! – Christianity, Hinduism, Mohammedanism, Jainism, Buddhism...three hundred religions in the world. You can choose your own kind of neurosis; they come in all shapes, in all sizes. You can easily pick any kind of fanaticism, neurosis, and that will keep you engaged your whole life – but simply engaged. It will not give you time or space to dance, to sing, to celebrate.

All kinds of goals basically create deep down in you a split – hypocrisy. You are that which you are, and you start trying to be that which you are not. In the beginning it is only an effort to be that which you are not; slowly, slowly you start pretending that you are becoming that which you are not, because to encounter failure continuously is very humiliating. At least you can pretend to others, you can wear masks, you can create a certain persona, a personality, a garb, a facade, and you can start living behind that facade. And people will look only at your mask and they will believe it. Once they start believing it, you will start believing it – because they are believing that you are holy, that you are saintly, that you are this and you are that.

It is a very strange game: you start it, and soon you will be caught in it yourself – in your own lie! Once you are caught in your own lie you will try to hide the truth, to evade the truth, to repress the truth; you will begin investing more and more in your lie. You may be a marigold and you may invest your whole life in being a rose. You may be a rose and you may invest your whole life in being a diamond – which you cannot be. This is the sheer stupidity of the experience humanity has been living with for centuries.

Hence what I say hurts. It is not a question of small dimensions; it is a question of immense dimensions. For thousands of years man has lived a hypocritical life, utterly false, pseudo, and now to shatter his whole investment, to shatter his whole mind, certainly hurts. Hence everybody is going to be against me except for just a few people who are intelligent enough to wake up.

"My so-called liberal mother is really such a prude," the high school cheerleader sadly told her locker partner. "She said that I could only pet with my dates if they didn't touch me below the waist."

"Oh, that's too bad," her schoolmate commiserated. "What do you intend to do about it?"

"Well," the cheerleader giggled, "the first thing I'm going to do is learn to stand on my head."

That's what your religious people have been doing: *sirshasana* – the art, the yoga of standing on your head. It certainly fulfills something: the ego. Whenever you can do something unnatural or at least pretend that you are doing it, it fulfills the ego. Nature cannot fulfill the ego. If you eat and enjoy eating, what is there to brag about? If you make love and you enjoy it, what is there to brag about? But if you become a celibate then there is something to brag about; if you fast then you have something which nobody else has. Then you can feel superior, higher, greater, bigger, *chosen*. The unnatural has an attraction – although it destroys your whole life – but the attraction is in the ego. And unless we drop this whole game of the ego, hypocrisy cannot disappear from the world.

Rabbi Goldstein had just moved into his apartment and decided he should get acquainted with his neighbor across the hall. When the door was opened, he was pleasantly surprised to be confronted by a young damsel considerably more than passably fair and considerably less than fully clad.

Though justifiably flustered by this smiling apparition, the rabbi nevertheless managed a remark singularly appropriate to the occasion: "Hi, I'm your new sugar across the hall – can I borrow a cup of neighbor?"

You can try to be unnatural, but your nature will assert itself in a thousand and one ways; it will come up again and again. You will have to hush it; you will have to repress it.

It was eight a.m. at a Las Vegas gambling palace and two lone bettors were still standing by a dice table awaiting further competition, when a lusciously endowed brunette attired in a suit happened by.

"Although it's quite early in the day," she announced, "I feel lucky this morning. I'd like to roll the dice once for twenty thousand dollars. Would the two of you care to take me up on the wager?"

"Sure, lady," answered one of the men, "we'll take your action."

"I hope you gentlemen won't mind," she then said, "but the only way I can get lucky is to roll the dice without my panties on."

So saying, the lissome lovely proceeded to remove her slacks and panties. With a shout of "Mamma needs a new pair of pants!" she rolled the dice, gave a squeal of delight and yelled, "I win!" She then picked up her money, her slacks and her underwear and made a hasty exit from the room.

The two men exchanged double takes, and one of them blurted out, "Hey, what did she roll anyway?"

"How the hell should I know?" snapped the other. "I thought *you* were watching the dice!"

We have created such a strange humanity – the whole rationale of all this mad earth, this mad humanity, is religious, spiritual. Search for the truth, search for God, search for the peaks, and you have lost yourself in the search.

There is only one search – to find yourself – and for that you need not go anywhere else. For that you have to withdraw from all your desires, ambitions, goals. You have to come back home.

You are not to become me. I am not your enemy – I cannot tell you to become me. If you try to become me you will only be a carbon copy, a hypocrite, you will only be an imitation.

Those who have gathered around me are not my followers, not my imitators – just companions, fellow celebrants, dance partners! Existence to me is a carnival; it is just a festival. It is for those who know how to dance. And the dance need not wait for tomorrow – tomorrow never comes – the dance has to be now, here, this very moment. This very silence has to become the dance!

So don't hanker for any peaks, just be where you are totally, utterly, and the goose is out! Hanker for the peaks, and the goose is in the bottle. Those peaks are the bottle, those goals are the bottle. They keep you encapsulated; they keep you imprisoned. The future is your bondage and the present is your freedom.

Here I differ totally from Jesus, from Buddha, from Krishna, from Mahavira, from everybody else. Knowingly, unknowingly, they have created a pattern of imitation for humanity. I want to destroy this whole pattern, this whole status quo. I want you to be just yourself. Whatsoever you are, you are beautiful as you are; you need not be somebody else to be beautiful.

That's the only way to enjoy, but it is up to you. If you want to suffer...and there are people who love suffering, they cannot live without suffering; their only joy is in suffering and more suffering. The more they suffer the more they feel that they are doing something great. Then it is up to you; don't make any fuss about it, then go to the peaks. But the peaks won't satisfy you, because from those peaks you will again be looking far ahead for further peaks.

The headmistress of a girls' boarding school was abruptly awakened one night by one of her students, a rather mature-looking sixteen-year-old. "Miss Forbes," she cried, "I've just been raped!"

"Now, be calm, Melissa," the headmistress told her firmly. "The first thing you must do is to go to the refrigerator and eat half a lemon."

"Half a lemon?" asked the surprised student. "Will that keep me from getting pregnant?"

"No," admitted the headmistress, "but it *will* get rid of that silly grin."

That's what religious people have been doing: removing all your smiles, making you look as sad as possible, as long-faced as possible.

Christians say Jesus never laughed. If it is true, then whatsoever he has said is wrong. If what he has said is right then this cannot be true, because the man continuously says, "Rejoice! I say to you again and again rejoice!" And Christians say he never laughed! Laughter seems to be mundane for them, laughter seems to be worldly; it is not good for holy people. Holy people have to be continuously sad; hence they have created a long tradition of sad, ill, sick, pathological people whom they worship.

The more pathological you look the more you will be worshipped. The more you are a sadist and a masochist the more you will be worshipped. Torture yourself and teach others to torture themselves – they call it asceticism – become a monk, renounce the world...

The word *monk* means one who lives alone, escapes from people. In fact it is in relationships where you find the opportunities to grow; it is love that is a challenge to growth; it is friendship that brings you to your real flavor. It is life – in all its adventures and challenges – that helps you to become mature, integrated.

Monks remain retarded; they remain stupid. They are bound to remain stupid – they have been taken out of the soil of life. At the most they are greenhouse plants: bring them into the world and they will immediately shrink and die. They are very afraid people, continuously trembling, afraid of hell, which does not exist, greedy for heaven, which does not exist – and between hell and heaven missing everything that exists.

The inexperienced young man had heard that a good way to

arouse sexual desire in a girl, who proved impervious to the more usual forms of wooing, was to forthrightly place her hand on his organ. Having parked with a date for more than an hour in the local lovers' lane with nothing to show for it but some sisterly kisses, he decided to try this new technique. The response was instantaneous: the girl berated him with the longest stream of invectives he had ever heard. Stunned, he tried to reply, but she refused to listen, insisting instead that he take her home at once.

As he pulled up in front of her house, she again started shouting imprecations. Finally out of breath, she demanded, "Well, do you have anything to say for yourself?"

"Yes, I have," was his pained reply. "Please let go."

The second question:

Osho,
I am a homosexual Catholic and badly suffer from stuttering. Can you help me out of my mess?

The first thing you should get out of is your Catholicism; that is the real mess. Homosexuality is not such a big problem; it is not a problem at all, in fact. It is part of the human freedom. There is nothing wrong if two persons choose a certain style of sexual relationship; it should be nobody's business. But the priests and the politicians are poking their noses into everything! They create guilt in you – absolutely unnecessary.

If two men are in love, what is wrong in it? What harm are they doing to anybody? In fact, they look happier than the heterosexuals; that's why they are called "gay." This is strange: I never see lesbians looking gay – they look sad, they look very serious – but homosexuals always look very gay, very sweet, real honeys.

I have been wondering what the matter is, why are lesbians not so happy? Maybe they cannot enjoy nagging, which has been an eternal joy for women. In fact, without their nagging I don't think anybody would ever have become religious. All your saints are the by-product of nagging. All your saints should be immensely grateful to women: they have driven their mates to be spiritual! There was no possibility left for them *in* the world; they had to escape to the monasteries. They say they are going in search of God; in fact, they are simply going away from the wife. They are cowards.

Lesbians don't look very happy. Something is missing, and that something seems to be that they cannot torture each other. They understand each other perfectly well, and because they understand each other very well there is no mystery left.

Men live in the head, women live in the heart. The heart can rejoice only when there is something very mysterious, something like a koan – the goose in the bottle. Neither does the bottle have to be broken nor the goose killed, and it has to be taken out too. The heart enjoys the mysterious. The head is not interested in the mysterious; it is interested in the act of puzzling, of riddling. Any riddle, any puzzle, interests the head. The approach of the head is logical.

To men women are mysterious; to connect with the woman a man must come to his heart, and he lives in his head. Hence the woman always remains a problem. He cannot understand her; he cannot explain what is happening; he cannot explain it away either. He has to live with a mystery, and that is a constant pain in his neck; it is beyond his grasp.

But with two men things are simple: both are logical. They understand the language, they understand logic; they understand mathematics, calculation. At the most a man is just a new question to be solved – not a mystery to be lived but a question to be solved; a problem which can be solved, which is not impossible to solve. That keeps two men interested, keeps them intrigued. Hence I see homosexuals looking gay. Lesbians looking very sad.

One more thing happens: homosexuals become more feminine and they start having a certain beauty, a certain "niceness" about them, a certain roundness, a grace. The lesbian becomes more manly; she starts losing her feminine grace; she becomes masculine, aggressive, hard. Hence, if you were a woman it would have been a problem, and I would have helped you to come out of it. But you are a man. Why bother? Why make much out of a simple thing? If you are enjoying a relationship with a man, enjoy it!

The Christian God himself seems to be homosexual – the whole trinity consists of three men. How they are managing it nobody knows – not a single woman! Only the Holy Ghost is a little suspect; maybe the Holy Ghost is bisexual? Ghosts can do any kind of thing! Otherwise the Father and the Son and the Holy Ghost – what kind of trinity is this? It is very homosexual! They have not allowed a single woman to be in it, just to keep out of trouble. One woman would have destroyed the whole trinity; it would have become a real triangle!

Homosexuality is not a problem. We should start looking at real problems and should not be concerned about unreal problems. There are real problems to be solved. It is a trick of the human mind – to create unreal problems so that you become occupied with them while real problems go on growing. This is an old strategy: politicians, priests, so-called religious leaders go on giving you pseudo problems to solve so that you become occupied with the pseudo.

The problem in itself is meaningless; the problem is not a problem at all, but how much fuss has gone on down the ages about homosexuality! There are countries where people are still killed for homosexual acts, murdered, sentenced to jail for their whole lives. Strange world! This is a twentieth-century world? Homosexuality is not a problem at all; there are thousands of real problems to be solved. But man has to be kept engaged with toys.

My effort is to withdraw all your attention from toys so that you can focus on the real problems of life; and if you focus on the real problems of life they can be solved. I don't see how homosexuality becomes a problem. How does it become a problem? Why should it be of concern to anybody? A love affair is two individuals' private concern; it is *their* intimacy, it is not a social phenomenon.

In fact, it will help the world population if more people turn homo-sexual. It will be good, very good for the world: less people will be born, the earth will be less burdened; there will be less poverty. Of course, less orphans and less Mother Teresas! There will be less need for contraceptives, birth control methods, sterilization, and of course the whole business of the Polack Pope will go out of his hands. That is his whole business! For one year continuously he has been talking against contraceptives, against birth control, sterilization, abortion. Homosexuality can solve all these problems simply!

So I don't see that there is much of a problem in it. The only problem is your Catholicism.

Rodney, the eldest son of a respectable Boston family, announced to his shocked father that he intended to live openly with his swishy boyfriend on Beacon Hill.

"Damn it, Rodney," the parent responded, "our family came over with John Winthrop, and we have never had a scandal such as this."

"I can't help it, father, I love him."
"But for God's sake, son, he's a Catholic!"

That is the true problem! Come out of your Catholicism. And when I say come out of your Catholicism, I mean come out of all kinds of stupid ideologies – Hindu, Mohammedan, Christian. Come out of ideologies and start living life as if you are Adam and Eve, the first man on the earth, the first woman on the earth. Start afresh, from scratch.

As far as your stuttering is concerned, what is wrong with it? It may just be because you have made such a problem out of homosexuality that you are stuttering. Stuttering – I have watched it in many people – comes in a state of stress, tension.

When I was a student in the university, my neighbor...a young man, a beautiful man, healthy, in every way intelligent. I had never seen him stuttering. Once his father visited him, and he immediately started stuttering in front of his father. I could not believe what was happening. The moment the father left he was perfectly okay. I asked him about it.

He said, "This is a problem. When I go back home, I cannot avoid stuttering in front of my father and mother. It happens...the more I try to avoid it the more it happens. Even when my father's letter comes and I start reading it, I suddenly feel a trembling. I cannot read my father's letter without stuttering. Otherwise I am perfectly okay."

So I said to him, "So it is not a question of stuttering; there is some stress, some tension. Your father is heavy to you, and you regress back to your childhood, back to your old fears, and those fears start overcoming your intelligence." I said to him, "Do one thing: next time your father comes, try to stutter with every word!"

He said, "How is that going to help?"

I said, "Try it. Don't try *not* to stutter; on the contrary try to stutter. Make every effort that not a single word should come out without stuttering!"

He said, "What are you suggesting? I have been doing just the opposite and have failed utterly. Your method seems to be such that it is bound to create more troubles for me!"

I said, "Give it a try."

The father came, and I was there, and he tried it – and he could not stutter!

There are a few things which happen only if you are trying; there are a few things which happen only if you *don't* try. The very effort comes out of fear and if fear is the cause then the effort cannot help. Hypnotherapists call it "the law of reverse effect."

If you are learning to ride a bicycle you may be on a sixty-foot-wide road, absolutely empty, nobody on the road, and then you see a milestone by the side of the road, and suddenly your cycle starts moving toward that milestone for no reason at all. You start feeling afraid; you try to avoid the milestone. Now, on a sixty-foot-wide road even a blind man has only a rare chance of hitting the milestone, but you will try hard, and the more you try the more you will become focused. Now the whole road disappears, there is only that milestone standing there like Hanumanji, the monkey god, giggling at you, making faces at you, attracting you like a magnetic force. You are doing everything to avoid it, but you are going...you know you are going. It is unavoidable! The more unavoidable you feel it is, the more energy you put into it. You become tense. The whole world has shrunk to Hanumanji...and the crash!

This is one of the fundamental laws of life. Homosexuality may seem to be the cause, but it is not homosexuality really; it is your attitude toward it, your approach to it. You are making a problem out of it; then there will be trouble.

My suggestion is: stutter beautifully – make stuttering songs! You will enjoy, others will enjoy, and that's what we are here for.

"Have faith and ye shall be healed!" intoned the evangelist at the revival meeting. A woman on crutches and a man came forward. The evangelist asked, "What is your name, my good woman?"

"I'm Mrs. Smith," she answered, "and I haven't been able to walk without crutches for twenty years."

"Well, Mrs. Smith," he said, "go behind that screen and pray."

Turning to the man, he asked, "What is your name?"

"My name ith Thamuelth," he answered, "and I have alwayth thpoken with a lithp."

"Alright, Mr. Samuels," the evangelist said, "go behind that screen with Mrs. Smith and pray."

After several minutes had passed, the revivalist announced, "I think the time has come. Witness these miracles. Mrs. Smith, throw your left crutch over the screen." The audience gasped as it sailed over. "Mrs. Smith, throw your right crutch over the screen." The crowd cheered as the second crutch appeared.

Encouraged, the evangelist commanded, "Mr. Samuels, say something in a loud, clear voice, so we can all hear you."

Samuels answered, "Mithuth Sthmith jutht fell on her ath!"

So what is wrong with it? It is a far greater miracle! So don't be worried about unnecessary things. Stutter joyously, enjoy it, and there is a possibility that you may stop stuttering – beware of it! If you don't want to stop it, then don't listen to me, you just go on trying not to stutter.

My suggestion is stutter, and don't be a miser. Fill the whole place with stuttering! Whomsoever you meet, stutter – don't miss an opportunity. Even the words that you can speak well, don't speak well, stutter! And you may be surprised that once you relax, once you start enjoying, once the tension is dropped, stuttering may disappear. If it disappears, good; if it does not disappear there is no harm in it. It is innocent!

Take life as easily as possible. But people don't understand me. I say to them, "Life is a mystery. It is not to be solved but to be lived." And somebody has asked me, "Osho, when you said that, I heard, 'Life is a *misery*, not to be solved but to be lived.'" That is up to you. To me it is a mystery, not to be solved but to be lived, but you can hear it as "misery."

Don't make unnecessary problems for yourself, so that your whole energy can become focused on the essential problem. And the essential problem is only one: Know thyself.

The third question:

Osho,
I am immensely interested in going to the moon. This longing has always haunted me as long as I can remember. Can you tell me one or two jokes about the moon?

Perhaps that's why you have come to me – my name means the moon. You are moonstruck; that means you are a lunatic! *Lunatic* simply means struck by the moon...and this is a gathering of mad people. You have come to the moon!

Your long-cherished desire is fulfilled – the goose is out!
But I have two jokes for you:

Shortly after his spaceship landed on the moon, the astronaut
debarked and began exploring the strange new terrain. He had
walked for only fifteen minutes when he came upon a lovely young
moon girl who was busily stirring an empty pot with a stick.

"Hi," he said, introducing himself, "I'm an astronaut here to discover things about the moon."

The moon girl stopped stirring long enough to throw him quite a
pleasant smile. "How nice it is that you are formed just like our moon
men," she observed. Throwing off her clothes, she asked, "And am I
structured as are Earth women?"

"Yes, you are," answered the now excited astronaut. "But tell
me, why do you stir that pot?"

"I'm making a baby," she said. And, sure enough, a few minutes
later a baby appeared in the pot.

"Now would you like to see how we make babies on Earth?"
asked the astronaut. The girl agreed, and the astronaut proceeded
with his passionate demonstration.

"That was enjoyable," she said afterward, "but where is the baby?"

"Oh, that takes nine months," explained the astronaut.

"Nine months?" she asked. "Then why did you stop stirring?"

A small group of scientists had spent an enlightening week on
the moon comparing life there with our own.

"Tell me," one Earth scientist asked his moon counterpart, "just
how do you reproduce the species here on this planet?"

"I shall be pleased to demonstrate," replied the leader of the
moon group, and he called forth a voluptuous moon beauty with
three heads. They then engaged their tentacles for a few moments,
and almost at once a small pouch began to form on the female's
back; it grew, and within little more than a minute it opened up very
much like a blooming flower, and a small moon child dropped out, as
fully developed as the adults but much smaller, and began scam-
pering about the room.

Once the Earth scientists had recovered from this unexpected
experience they attempted to explain how procreation differs in
our world. The Moonians insisted upon being shown, and after

unsuccessful attempts to dissuade them, the chief scientist of the expedition finally agreed. Choosing a comely scientific aide from the group, he took her to a cot in the corner of the room and there proceeded to make love to her in a manner to which we here on Earth are more accustomed.

The Moonians examined the couple from every angle, and when they were finished, their leader said, "That was certainly unusual and, I must say, interesting, but where is the baby – or was the demonstration a failure?"

"It is difficult to say," replied the Earth scientist. "We cannot tell at once. But if the contact was successful, then the baby will arrive in approximately nine months."

"Nine months!" exclaimed the Moonian. "Amazing! But tell us then, doctor, if the Earth child will not be born for nine months, why were you in such a hurry there at the end?"

Enough for today.

transcendence brings buddhahood

The first question:

Osho,
Why do Indians think of sex in terms of need instead of fun? They
also think at the same time that they have transcended sex, but in
reality it has only been suppressed. Is there any similarity between
suppression and transcendence which can mislead people, as you
sometimes say that there is some similarity between a buddha and
a madman?

Indian culture is the most rotten culture that has evolved in the
world, the rottenest – rotten to the very core. It is so rotten that it
has forgotten how to die. To die one needs to be a little bit alive,
and unless you know how to die you simply vegetate, you stagnate.

Death is a process of revival. Just as each individual has to die
to be born again, each culture has to die to be born again. Each
society, each civilization has to pass through life to death, from death
to life again.

Indian culture is the only culture which has not died for thousands of years. There have been many cultures in the world: the

Assyrian, the Babylonian, the Greek, the Roman, the Egyptian. They all flowered, blossomed: they contributed their beauty to the world – their sculpture, their music, their poetry, their drama – and then they disappeared without leaving a trace behind. This is how it should be.

If all the old people in your family were alive – your father and your father's father and his father's father to the very end, to Adam and Eve and God the Father – then one thing is certain: you would be crushed. So many old people, all corpses, are enough to crush a small child who is delicate like a rose.

One of the greatest things that Friedrich Nietzsche did was to declare: God is dead and man is free.

God as father has to be dead, otherwise his weight will be too much, it will be too mountainous. It won't allow the freshness of humanity. It won't allow exploration, it won't allow adventure. The old man will be too cautious, too cunning, too calculating, too Jewish. His whole experience of the past will be enough to destroy the child. The child needs exploration; and, of course, when you explore you commit many mistakes – that is part of growth. One should be allowed to commit mistakes. One should certainly be intelligent enough not to commit the same mistakes again and again; one should be creative enough to invent new mistakes. That's the way one expands, grows. That's the way consciousness becomes integrated.

Life is a trial-and-error process. The old man drops all mistakes, errors. He becomes so accustomed to doing the right thing that exploration, adventure, disappear from his life. And because of his own fears he won't allow the new generations to go in new directions, in new dimensions. He will make them afraid; he will paralyze them, he will cripple them. That's what has been happening in India.

India is a strange case. It is extraordinary in a way: this has never happened anywhere else. All the countries, all the cultures, civilizations, have lived, died and were resurrected again; India has remained the same. It is more like a plastic flower than like a real rose. It is more concerned with stability than with aliveness. Its whole concern is how to go on and on forever.

But that is not the real thing. How to live each moment totally is the question. It is not a question of endurance; the question is one of depth. Only those who live in depth know what life is all about. Those who live in endurance live horizontally, superficially. Their life is a mask; there is no authenticity in it. Hence, I say Indian culture is neither alive nor dead but living in a kind of suspension, in a kind of limbo. It is a ghost culture: all that is significant, all that makes life a joy, has been dropped because it is dangerous, and all that is stable, permanent, plastic, has been gathered together because it is safer.

Remember, this is the way of an old man. The old man always thinks of safety, security, his bank balance; he always thinks in terms of fear, because death is always standing in front of him.

The child never bothers about death; his concern is life. He is interested in going into the uncharted, into the unknown; he is ready to take risks. Those who are ready to risk, they are the only truly alive ones. They may not live long, but that is not the point at all. To live for a single moment with authenticity, totality, integrity is more than enough. A single moment of total experience is far greater than the whole of eternity. It contains the whole of eternity, it contains timelessness. But one can go on vegetating for thousands of years like a cabbage, a cauliflower – very holy looking, very saintly.

Cabbages are not sinners, and cauliflowers are great scholars. A cabbage becomes a cauliflower through college education. Cauliflowers are pundits, theologians, religious people. This country is full of these people, and the burden of them is great. Somebody needs to help this country to die so that it can live again. Crucifixion is a basic condition for resurrection. The art of living is preceded by the art of dying.

This country is stinking, it has nothing else to brag about, so it brags about the past. It brags about its phoniness, it brags about its holiness, it brags about its spirituality – which is all nonsense because the basic foundation is missing. We talk about the temple – the temple is possible, but first you have to put the basic foundation together.

Life is a hierarchy of needs. First the physical has to be taken care of; material existence has to be taken care of. Science fulfills a basic need. If you miss science you will miss religion. Between science and religion is the world of art. These are the three basic dimensions of life. Science has to take care of the material, the physiological, the biological – the external needs of man. Religion has to take care of the innermost – interiority, subjectivity. Between the two is the world of aesthetics: art, poetry, music, dance, drama, literature.

A man who is hungry cannot think of poetry. A man who is hungry cannot conceive of meditation. It is impossible! This long, long traditional ego tries to hide its poverty. The so-called Indian spiritualism, the so-called desire of the Indian culture to guide the whole world toward spirituality is just stupid. It is sheer nonsense, it is rubbish. But that is their only face-saving device – they can save face only behind that screen. They know their bodies are hungry, they know that things which are absolutely necessary to them are not available. They are starving; they are ill, sick in every way. Eighty percent of the country is living as beggars. Few are well nourished: almost everybody is undernourished. When a person is undernourished it is not only the body that suffers, remember; undernourishment in a very subtle way destroys the capacity of your mind.

Mind needs its own nourishment, and unless the body is adequately nourished the mind cannot be nourished. First the body's needs have to be fulfilled. When there is something more after the body's fulfillment, then nourishment goes to the brain cells. The mind is a luxury that does not exist in animals; it is a human prerogative. It came into existence only because man could manage his bodily needs so totally that there was energy left, and that overflowing energy became his brain, became his mind, became his psychology.

When psychological needs are fulfilled, totally fulfilled, and again there is more energy available, that energy transforms into spirituality, into meditation, into buddhahood.

India is in a sad state, and the saddest thing is that Indians try to hide it rather than expose it. They are angry at me because I am exposing the truth as it is. They are angry at me because I am not trying to cover it up. They would like me, they would respect me, they would call me a great mahatma, an incarnation of God and all kinds of rubbish, under the condition that I go on covering their wounds.

I cannot cover anybody's wounds. I can heal them, but the healing process is a totally different process. First you have to expose your wounds to the sun, to the air. You have to expose them. It hurts! Wounds which have been kept secret for thousands of years, suddenly exposed... You cannot believe it. You have always believed that you are great spiritualists, but I see the whole phoniness of it; I see the hypocrisy of it. The greatest hypocrisy that happens happens through two denials: food and sex. These are basic needs, and they are two sides of the same coin. They are not very different.

Food is needed for the existence of the individual. An individual can exist without sex. It will not be much of a joy, but he can survive. Without food the individual cannot exist; he will shrink and die. At the most, if he is perfectly healthy, he can exist without food for three months – ninety days – but that too only if he is perfectly healthy, and if he has too much extra food accumulated in his body in the form of fat and other things. Then he can survive for three months.

That survival, remember, has nothing to do with religion; that is sheer cannibalism – one is eating oneself. When you fast you are eating your own meat, hence I am against fasting; that is the worst kind of meat-eating. You can fast and every day you will lose weight. Where is that weight disappearing to? You are digesting it. Within three months you will die.

The individual can exist for a little while without food, he can exist without sex – he can survive – but the human race, the species, cannot exist without sex. That is food for the species. Sex is food for the species. Without sex humankind will disappear. And the people who have been teaching celibacy are murderous. The people who have been teaching celibacy to humanity are basically cutting the very roots of humanity. If they were to be followed literally there would be no humanity left.

There would have been no Mahavira, no Buddha, no Krishna; there would have been no Mohammed, no Kabir, no Nanak, if their parents had followed the idea of celibacy. It is good, it is fortunate that Buddha's father did not follow the stupid idea of celibacy, otherwise the world would have missed one of the greatest flowerings.

If celibacy is perpetuated, then humanity will disappear. It is a very egoistic idea, egoistic in the sense that you only care about yourself. Indians go on talking about spirituality, selflessness, and at the same time, with the same face, they go on talking about celibacy. Celibacy is selfishness, absolute selfishness. Your parents and their parents and their parents have all joined together to give birth to you. Now, trying to be celibate, forcing celibacy, simply means you are closing the doors to future humanity. And you call it selflessness? You call it spirituality?

This is pure egoism – as if you were the center of the whole existence, as if the whole existence existed only for you: because you have been produced, now there is no need for anything; the whole can disappear.

Although the teaching continues, nobody follows it. Unnatural teachings cannot be followed. That is one good thing about them. Only a few fools, maniacs, obsessed people may try to follow them, but any man of intelligence will not follow such ideas.

Such ideas create two kinds of difficulties. One: those who are cunning, they become hypocrites. And those who are innocent, they become guilty. That's what has happened in India, and the same has happened on a wider scale all over the world. The disease is contagious. It must have started in India; its origin seems to be Indian. That is the only contribution that India has made to the world – a contagious disease which creates hypocrites and guilty people. Both are ugly specimens. The world needs neither the hypocrites nor the guilty.

The hypocrites become priests, monks, mahatmas, sages, saints, and the guilty become the followers. This is the game that is going on.

You ask me: "Why do Indians think of sex in terms of need...?" Because their needs are not fulfilled. They are in all kinds of need – to them sex is also a need. A needy person has an eye which projects his needs everywhere. You see only that which you can see, you hear only that which you can hear: you are continuously choosing according to your need. To a hungry person a beautiful woman simply looks like a delicious dish. The very idea shows where the man stands.

There are expressions in all the languages of the world for love. People have started using words like *eating* – "I would like to eat you" the lover says to the woman. What kind of love is this? Lovers bite each other, lovers chew each other – as if they are chewing gum. Lovers leave tooth marks on each other. What kind of poetry is this? They scratch each other with their nails... Is this love or is something else masquerading behind it?

Love should be deep caring. One should not think in terms of food, of eating, biting – these are ugly expressions.

India lives with all kinds of needs. Hence, sex also becomes only a need, at the most, a release, a tranquilizer – the same kind of release that you feel when you have a good sneeze: some burden, some tension is gone. But there is no fulfillment in it, there is no rejoicing in it.

Indians make love as if they are thieves, as if they are doing something wrong. They make love as if they are going against God, as if they are committing some sin.

Of course they have to make love because that is a need. It can only be a need when their other needs are fulfilled. When all the needs are fulfilled, love starts having a totally different dimension to it – the dimension of fun, the dimension of dance and music. Then you are not using it as a relaxation, as a tranquilizer, as a sneeze – you start sharing. Love becomes more prominent; sex becomes secondary. When it is a need love is just a word: sex is the only thing, the reproductive activity is the only thing.

You know it – it is a well-known fact scientifically observed all over the world – that poor people produce more children. Why? They don't have any other ways of entertaining themselves. They don't have the idiot box, the TV, they cannot sit glued in their chair for six hours. They don't have a chair, in fact! They don't have the money to go to a hotel to participate in some celebration, to go to a movie, to drink alcohol, to dance, sing... All possibilities are closed. The tiredness of the day, the routine of work, the continuity of the same rut... The only possibility, a free amusement available to them, is sex. That becomes their last act in the day. So before going to sleep they religiously devote one, two minutes to it, and then they fall asleep like a log.

The newly-married couple were entertaining a bachelor in the den of their suburban home when the conversation turned to sexual morality.

"Since you claim to be so liberal," the Indian bachelor challenged the husband, "would you let me kiss your wife's breasts for a thousand dollars?"

Not wishing to seem prudish, and needing the extra money, the couple agreed, and the wife removed her blouse and bra. Then pressing his face between her breasts the chap nestled there for several minutes, until the husband grew impatient to complete the deal. "Go ahead and kiss them," he urged the bachelor.

"I would love to," the fellow sighed, "but I really can't afford it."

The question is whether you can afford anything else... Hence, to the Indian mind, sex remains an animal act. It never rises to the realms of poetic beauty, it never becomes love. So whenever you talk to the Indian about love, he immediately thinks you are talking about sex. *Love* is immediately, automatically translated as *sex*. It is impossible to talk to the Indian about love. This is my experience of talking to millions of Indians all over the country. Talk about love, and by the time the word reaches them it is no longer *love*, it becomes *sex*.

They know only sex. Love has no other connotation for them. It is such a misunderstanding, one feels almost helpless. Talking to Indians is really troublesome.

You can talk about God, you can talk about the soul, you can talk about *moksha*, nirvana; you can talk about the Vedas, and there will be no misunderstanding, because they are like parrots – for thousands of years they have been repeating those words. Not that they will understand you, but at least they will understand the words. When you say "God" they know its meaning. They don't know the experience, but at least the meaning is known. But when you talk about love, even the meaning is not known. The experience of it is far, far away.

She had just finished her shower when the doorbell rang. Tiptoeing to the front door, shivering in plump, pink nudity, she called, "Who is it?"

"The blind man," came a mournful voice.

So she shrugged and opened the door with one hand while reaching for her purse with the other. When she turned to face the man he was grinning from ear to ear. And she saw that he was holding a large package in his arms.

"You can see!" she exclaimed.

"Yeah," he nodded happily, "and mighty pretty too. Now, where do you want I should put these blinds?"

The romantic young man sat on the park bench with a first date. He was certain his charming words and manner would win her as they had so many others.

"Some moon out tonight," he cooed.

"There certainly is," she agreed.

"Some really bright stars in the sky."

She nodded.

"Some dew on the grass."

"Some do!" she said indignantly. "But I am not that sort!"

It is really difficult to talk with Indians about love: they have never lived the experience. All that they know is the sexual mechanism, and all that they know is sexual animalness; that is their experience. They cannot understand sex as fun – because sex cannot be fun, only love can be fun.

Love is fun: it is a play, it is playfulness. And at the ultimate peak of love, the same playfulness becomes prayerfulness.

These are the three stages: need, playfulness, prayerfulness. Unless you have experienced love at its ultimate, utmost peak as prayer, you have not really lived your life; you have missed the point.

You say: "Why do Indians think of sex in terms of need instead of fun?" They don't know anything about fun, about playfulness. They are serious people – very holy, very spiritual. They are walking corpses. You cannot expect playfulness from them; you can expect only long faces.

You cannot live with saints for long. Even to be with a saint for twenty-four hours is a punishment; it is not a reward because within twenty-four hours he will make you so bitter toward life, he will make you so sad, he will make you so sour, he will make you feel guilty, condemned... That is his only joy. Religious people only enjoy one thing: making everybody sad, taking away people's laughter.

They condemn me because I am teaching people laughter. I am teaching people love; I am teaching people how to rejoice in the moment, in the very ordinariness of life. There is no other kind of life anywhere; there is no other world; this is the only world! And we have to live this world. We are not to sacrifice this world for some other world.

I am not teaching sacrifice, I am not teaching asceticism, I am not teaching fasting, I am not teaching celibacy. I am teaching the celebration of life. That's what they have been missing for thousands of years.

They cannot understand sex as fun; it is a misery. If they cannot understand it as fun, they cannot understand it as prayer; that is impossible.

You say: "They also think at the same time that they have transcended sex, but in reality it has only been suppressed." Transcendence of sex is possible only when sex reaches to the flowering of prayerfulness. Before that, sex cannot be transcended. You can only jump beyond sex from that borderline. Then it is not celibacy, it is simply the disappearance of the ego into the whole. It is not really transcendence of sex but becoming part of the whole orgasmic universe. It is reaching to the ultimate of union with the whole.

What are you doing when you are making love to a woman? You are trying to have a certain union with the opposite pole. For a moment the union happens – rarely, because so many conditions have to be fulfilled. Unless all conditions are fulfilled you may simply go through the gestures of making love. Only once in a while are a man and woman really in tune – at-one-ment, attunement – and then for a moment, the orgasmic joy.

What is orgasmic joy? The disappearance of the ego for a moment. But even for a moment it is tremendously significant, precious, far more precious than any Kohinoor. The same thing happens on a deeper level in prayer. With prayer you are not trying to meet with the other person, but you are trying to meet with the universe. The other person has become just a window. You are no longer attached to the window frame. You are going through the window into the world of the stars, clouds, birds. You are moving beyond. Love teaches you how to go beyond the window and to search for the stars. Once you have taken flight, the window is left far behind. Once you leave the window, a miracle happens. Because your ego was framed by the window: once you leave the window behind, your ego is also left behind. The ego needs the other: when the other is no longer there, the ego is also no longer there.

Psychologists say the ego comes later on. First, you start feeling the presence of the other. The child first feels the presence of mother, father, brothers, sisters, walls, paintings, whatsoever surrounds him. Slowly, slowly he becomes aware of the fact: "I am separate from all these. Sometimes Mother is there and sometimes she is not there, but I am always here." First enters the experience of the other, and then the ego arises.

In the same way in prayer – the reverse order – first there is the disappearance of the other and then the ego dissolves. Once you have left the frame, the small frame of the lover and the beloved, and you have taken yourself into the beyond, the dissolution happens. Buddha calls it nirvana. The word is beautiful: *nirvana* simply means cessation of the flame. Just as you extinguish a lamp and suddenly the flame disappears into the whole, so it is in the ultimate state of love. Then one knows transcendence. Transcendence of the ego becomes the transcendence of sex.

Remember, it is not against sex. In fact, you have moved your momentary experience of sex into cosmic sex; you have become one with the orgasm of existence itself. Now it will be there each moment, you cannot lose it. Now the goose is really out! You cannot enter the bottle again.

Transcendence of sex is a totally different phenomenon from the suppression of it. But suppression can give you the feeling that you have transcended.

The old maid rushed up to the policeman. "I have been raped! I have been attacked," she cried. "He ripped off my clothing; he smothered me with burning kisses. Then he made mad, passionate love to me!"

"Calm yourself, calm yourself, madam," said the officer. "Just when did all this take place?"

"Twenty-three years ago this September," said the woman.

"Twenty-three years ago?" he exclaimed. "How do you expect me to arrest anyone for something he did twenty-three years ago?"

"Oh, I don't want you to arrest anyone, officer," said the woman. "I just like to talk about it, that's all."

You will be surprised that all your so-called saints continuously talk against sex. Why? If they have transcended it, why this obsession with sex? In Indian scriptures you will find such obscene descriptions of women that you will be surprised. Your *Playboy*s and magazines like that are nothing by comparison. You can go and see the temples at Khajuraho, Konarak, Puri, and you will see that your so-called obscene literature is just the beginning. Khajuraho has the most obscene sculpture that has ever existed anywhere in the world. It took hundreds of years to do because it is stone sculpture; it is not just a photograph of a nude model in a *Playboy* magazine. Thousands of sculptors for hundreds of years must have worked on it; and not one temple, hundreds of temples. Why are these sculptures on the temples? What have temples got to do with it?

They have much to do with it. Saints need it, religious people need it. These are their fantasies. These are what they are seeing inside themselves; they want them to be projected. In Indian scriptures you will be surprised to note that Indian gods are the worst rapists in the world. They are not contented with heavenly beauties; they continue to descend to the earth and seduce and rape earthly women. They become tired of the heavenly beauties for the simple reason that heavenly beauties are a little stale, stale in the sense that they never grow old, they always remain the same. They don't perspire; hence they don't need a shower. Their bodies are not ordinary: they are made of gold and silver. Now what can you do with a woman with a body of gold and silver, eyes of emeralds and diamonds? Sooner or later you will get tired. It is a toy, a doll, it is not a woman. She never nags you; she never throws pillows at you. No drama, no life!

They descend to earth. All the Indian *devas* – the Indian gods – are very sexual, obsessively sexual. The saints who have been writing these scriptures describe women in such beautiful words. That shows their minds. But they are pretending at the same time that they are condemning sex, they are telling you these things so that you can remain aware of them.

The elderly spinster hired a young lawyer to prepare her will. "I have ten thousand dollars set aside," she explained, "and I want to spend it on myself. Nobody in this town has ever paid any attention to me, but they will sit up and take notice when I die."

Warming to the subject she cackled, "I want to spend all of eight thousand dollars on the biggest, fanciest funeral this town has ever seen."

"Well," said the lawyer, "that's a lot to pay for burying someone in these parts. But it is your money, madam, and you are entitled to spend it any way you like. Now, what about the other two thousand?"

"I'll take care of that," the old woman replied with a broad smile. "I've never been to bed with a man and I aim to try that at least once before I'm through. As you can see I'm not much to look at, but I figure for two thousand dollars I can get me a man that is young enough and handsome enough to please me."

That night the lawyer reported the conversation to his wife. As they discussed the situation, the wife casually mentioned how nice it would be to have the two thousand dollars. Minutes later they were on their way to the spinster's house, the wife driving. As the lawyer stepped from the car he instructed his wife, "Pick me up in two hours."

Returning at the prescribed hour, the wife tooted the horn. No response from the house. She then blew a prolonged blast. An upstairs window was raised and the lawyer thrust out his head. "Come back in four days," he shouted. "She's decided to let the municipal committee bury her."

These are the people, real people. Don't be deceived by their faces. Look deep inside them, and you will find tremendous madness.

Suppression brings madness; transcendence brings buddhahood.

Yes, I have said there is some similarity between a buddha and a madman. The similarity is that a buddha goes beyond the mind, and the madman falls below the mind. The same similarity exists between transcendence of sex and suppression of sex. Transcendence is going beyond sex – and to go beyond one has to go through; sex has to be used as a ladder – and suppression is falling below sex.

Suppression creates neurosis. Transcendence brings flowering, flowering of all that is best in you, flowering of all that is your real being. It is the release of your hidden splendor.

The second question:

Osho,
You said recently that you loved Wilhelm Reich. I have studied and written about him for years. While your ideas – sex equals energy, living in the now, and God is life – agree with his, you go far beyond him. In what way was he limited?

Edward Mann, I have read your book on Wilhelm Reich. I also remember you quoted me in that book.

Wilhelm Reich and my ideas have a certain superficial similarity, but remember it is superficial. Wilhelm Reich is a thinker, not a meditator, and sometimes thinkers groping in the dark can find a few things, they can stumble upon a few things. But to have eyes is a totally different phenomenon.

Yes, once in a while you can find the door by groping in the darkness – even a blind man can find it – but to have eyes, and to have light, and to go directly to the door without groping is a totally different phenomenon.

Wilhelm Reich is certainly appreciated by me, appreciated for the fact that he is not a meditator, and yet he has stumbled upon something which only meditators can come across. That is also his limitation: he is only a thinker. What he preaches he cannot practice. In fact he does just the opposite of it. His blindness can be seen in his life, not in his words.

Wilhelm Reich's wife wrote about him that he was a very jealous man. Now that is impossible. If a man has transcended sex, then jealousy is impossible. He continuously talked about getting rid of possessiveness, jealousy, but about his wife he was very suspicious. Finally they had to separate, and the cause of separation was Wilhelm Reich, himself. He meddled with all kinds of women continuously. He had many love affairs in the name of freedom, in the name of love, in the name of nonpossessiveness, in the name of friendship and sharing. But he wouldn't allow the same for his wife.

Even when he would leave his town, he told his friends to keep an eye on his wife. Wilhelm Reich's wife was herself a psychoanalyst. It was impossible for her to understand. But I can see why it happened – he was only a thinker.

Thinkers are, in a way, cunning. For themselves they find all kinds of excuses, but for others there is a totally different standard. That's where he was limited. Because he was not a meditator he could not transform his sexual energy into playfulness, prayerfulness, and ultimately into an orgasmic existence.

That's why he went mad. It is dangerous to play with fire. If you don't understand its nature it is better to leave it alone. Sex is fire because it is life: to play with it without understanding the whole process of its transformation is certainly dangerous. And that danger was what happened to him.

He was on the right path, but he was blind. He needed grounding in meditation. He would have become a buddha, but he became just a madman.

You say, "While your ideas – sex equals energy…" These are not my ideas, these are my experiences. A clear-cut distinction has to be understood. For Wilhelm Reich these are ideas. A blind man can have ideas about light, but that will not help him. A deaf man can have ideas about music, but that will not make him understand music, experience music. I don't have any ideas, these are my experiences. Whatsoever I am saying to you I am not saying it as a philosopher.

I am not a thinker at all; to me thinking is a very low-quality activity. What I am saying is my experiencing. So these are not my ideas on sex; these are actual experiences. I am not trying to indoctrinate you; I am simply inviting you to experience what I have experienced. So I don't ask you to believe in me.

Wilhelm Reich was a fanatic. He wanted his followers to believe in him, to believe in him absolutely. He was very dictatorial. He would not allow any doubt in anybody's mind, and he was constantly living in fear – fear of persecution, as if he were being persecuted continuously, as if somebody were after him. These are the signs of a fanatic mind.

He had the possibility of growing, but he needed the right soil. That was missing. Had he been one of my sannyasins, there would have been a totally different kind of man born out of him.

He lived in the bottle. The goose could not come out. He became too attached to the bottle – his ideology, his philosophy. And this constant fear of persecution, suspicion, drove him mad.

You say: "Your ideas – sex, living in the now, and God is life – agree with his…" They only appear to agree. Living in the now, how can you feel persecuted? Persecution is always going to be tomorrow. Right at this moment how can you feel persecuted? It can happen only in the next moment.

His whole life he was talking about living in the now, but it was only talk, mere talk; he never lived in the now. He was thinking of himself in the old foolish pattern, as being a prophet.

This stupid Judaic idea of being a prophet has tortured many people in the West. Christians, Mohammedans, Jews – all the three religions which were born outside India, have revolved around the idea of the prophet. Sigmund Freud had the same attitude, and Wilhelm Reich was a disciple of Sigmund Freud. Then Carl Gustav Jung had the same idea; he was also a follower of Sigmund Freud. Then Adler had the same idea; he was also a follower of Sigmund Freud. All by-products of the Jewish mind: they were all thinking in terms of the salvation of the whole of humanity depending on them.

That is living somewhere else, not in the now.

Just the other day, Sheela brought a report from a Christian theologian, a big report against me. He must have come with pre-conceived ideas, and got very confused. He could not manage with his preconceived ideas and he could not let go of them either. So he is wishy-washy: one thing he says against me, one thing he says for me. He has got into such a mess. But I liked one thing that he said – although he thought he was making a very significant criticism.

He said: "The moment Osho dies, his whole movement will disappear like a soap bubble." I loved it! That's how it should be! Why should it continue? What for? There is no reason. I live now; I am not interested in the future at all. What does it matter whether my movement disappears like a soap bubble or not? I love soap bubbles! They look beautiful in the sun. And they should disappear so that a few other people can make other soap bubbles. I have no monopoly over them. In fact, the world would have been better if the soap bubble that was created by Jesus had disappeared with him. Then these Polack Popes would not be here. Now they are making much fuss about a bubble which is not there. The soap bubble that Buddha created, had it disappeared, would have been a great blessing to humanity, because all these Buddhist monks and theologians, and all kinds of stupid people...we would have been saved from them!

Just the other day I was reading a Buddhist scripture. Buddhist scriptures say that there are thirty-three thousand rules for each Buddhist monk to follow. Thirty-three thousand rules! Even to remember them you will need a computer. What kind of rules? I will tell you just one rule. When a Buddhist monk goes to the toilet he should remove the lid of the toilet very slowly; no noise should be made. Why? Because there are always hungry ghosts who eat shit. If they eat your shit, *you* are responsible; then you will suffer in your future lives. Great people! Great religious rules!

This idea is of prophets who are trying to solve everybody's misery, who come for the salvation of humanity. There is no established fact that Jesus came, and yet Christians still go on bragging that he came for the salvation of humanity. But the salvation of humanity has not happened yet. Two thousand years have passed. He proved a very impotent prophet. What kind of salvation has happened? Jainas say that Mahavira came to uplift humanity. Humanity is where it is. Buddha came to deliver everybody...

I want to put a full stop to all this nonsense. I am not here to deliver anybody. Why should I deliver you? Your parents have already done that! I have no responsibility. I am not responsible to anybody – to any humanity, to any future. I am enjoying *my* moment, and those who want to enjoy this moment, this beautiful soap bubble in the sun, they can enjoy with me.

He thinks – the Christian theologian who came from Germany just to study what is happening here – that of course it looks beautiful now, but as Osho dies it will disappear.

It *should* disappear. I will make every arrangement for it to disappear. It should not remain even for a single moment, because that will be a dead thing.

Wilhelm Reich lived with this prophetic mission. All prophets are in a way mad, a little neurotic. Even good people, even people like Jesus, have a little strain of neurosis: "the only begotten son of

God." Just see the neurosis. So what are all the others, bastards? Jesus claims that he is born of a virgin mother. What nonsense! Some neurosis, some streak of neurosis! The slate is not absolutely clean...some hangover from the past. He was waiting for miracles. At the very last moment, on the cross, he was waiting. He shouted at God, "Why have you forsaken me?" You see the expectation? You see the demand? He is frustrated, he is angry: "Why have you forsaken me?" He must have been waiting deep down for a miracle to happen, expecting that God will descend and save his only begotten son. But no God descended, because there is no God. It was not possible. He was continually praying, raising his hands toward the sky, and calling, "*Abba*, Father." These are childish attitudes. But this is what has happened in the past.

With me it is a totally different phenomenon. I want to make a complete break from the past. I am not a prophet, I am not a messiah, I am not the only begotten son of God, I have not come to make arrangements for your salvation. There is no need – the goose is out!

Wilhelm Reich lived in reaction, not in rebellion. And the distinction is subtle. He was reacting. When you react against something you remain attached to it; you cannot be free of it. Reaction is a kind of negative attachment.

I am not reacting, I am simply disconnected. I am discontinuous with the past because that is the only way to live *now*. I have no past and no future. This moment is all!

The third question:

Osho,
I don't have any questions. Still there is one... Could you please say something crazy that has no purpose?

What do you think I have been doing all along? Do you think there is any purpose in what I am saying? Can you find a crazier man than me?

I am utterly crazy, and I have no purpose at all. I am just enjoying myself. I love to talk, so I love to talk... Hence, I have freedom which no thinker can ever have, because he has to be consistent. I don't care at all about any consistency. The moment I have said anything, it is finished; then I don't look back. I have never read any of my books – I don't even remember the names.

If somebody asks me, "Osho, You have said this in that book…" I say, "Really? It must have been said by somebody else. That man died long ago."

So everything that I am saying is purposeless, as purposeless as the roses, as a bird on the wing, as the stars, as the dewdrops in the early morning sun. What purpose could there be? I am not in any way purposive. It is sheer joy.

Three Polacks are standing outside a brothel discussing what prices they are willing to pay for the services inside. They decide that one of them should go inside first while the other two wait outside.

Half an hour later, the one who went inside comes out with a gleaming smile across his face.

"What happened? What was it like?" his friends ask.

"Well, I paid five zlotys, went into a room and this tall sexy woman was waiting for me. She took my clothes off, put two pineapple rings over my prick and proceeded to slowly eat them off. It was great!"

The second Polack, pleased with his friend's report, goes inside. An hour later he comes out, a big Cheshire cat grin on his face.

"What happened?" asked the other two.

"Well, I paid ten zlotys, and it was the same as our first friend. But this time she put four pineapple rings over my cock and ate them off very, very slowly."

The third Polack, by this time was very horny. He rushed into the brothel and came out fifteen minutes later with a long, sad face.

"Well," ask his friends, "what's wrong? What happened?"

"Well, begins the sad Polack, "it started off great. I paid twenty zlotys and she put six rings of pineapple over my cock, plus a big scoop of whipped cream."

"Wow!" the friends exclaim.

"That's not all," continues the third, "a handful of crushed nuts, a sugar wafer, hot chocolate sauce, and topped off with a beautiful red cherry."

"That sounds great," one of the others said. "What could possibly make you so sad then?"

"Well, it looked so fucking good, I ate it myself!"

Enough for today.

perfectly imperfect

The first question:

Osho,
Are you infallible?

I am infallibly fallible! First, I am not a perfectionist because to me perfectionism is the root cause of all neurosis. Unless humanity gets rid of the idea of perfection it is never going to be sane. The very idea of perfection has driven the whole of mankind to a state of madness. To think in terms of perfection means you are thinking in terms of ideology, goals, values, should's, should-not's. You have a certain pattern to fulfill, and if you fall from the pattern you will feel immensely guilty – a sinner. The pattern is bound to be such that you cannot achieve it. If you can achieve it then it will not be of much value to the ego.

The intrinsic quality of the perfectionist ideal is that it should be unattainable; only then is it worth attaining. You see the contradiction? That contradiction creates a schizophrenia: you are trying to do the impossible, which you know perfectly well is not going to happen – it cannot happen in the very nature of things. If it can happen then it is not much of a perfection; then anybody can do it. Then there is not much ego nourishment in it: your ego cannot chew on it, cannot grow on it. The ego needs the impossible and the impossible, by its very nature, is not going to happen. So only two alternatives are left: one is, you start feeling guilty. If you are innocent, simple, intelligent, you will start feeling guilty – and guilt is a state of sickness.

I am not here to create any guilt in you. My whole effort is to help you to get rid of all guilt. The moment you are free of guilt, rejoicing bursts forth. Guilt is rooted in the idea of perfection.

The second alternative is: if you are cunning then you will become a hypocrite, you will start pretending that you have achieved it. You will deceive others and you will even try to deceive yourself. You will start living in illusions, hallucinations, and that is very unholy, very irreligious, very unwholesome. To pretend, to live a life of pretensions, is far worse than the life of a guilty man. The guilty man at least is simple, but the pretender, the hypocrite, the saint, the so-called sage, the mahatma, is a crook. He is basically inhuman – inhuman to himself because he is repressing; that's the only way to pretend. Whatsoever he finds in himself which goes against perfection has to be repressed. He will be boiling within, he will be full of anger and rage. His anger and rage will come out in thousands of ways; in subtle ways, indirect ways, it will surface.

Even people like Jesus – nice, good – are full of anger, rage. And they are against such innocent things, you cannot believe.

Jesus comes followed by his followers, that bunch of fools they call apostles. He is hungry, that whole bunch is hungry. They come to a fig tree, and the fig tree is not in season. It is not its fault, but Jesus gets so angry that he condemns the fig tree, he curses the fig tree. Now, how is this possible? On the one hand he says, "Love thy enemy as thyself." On the other hand he cannot even forgive a fig tree which has no fruits because it is not the season.

This dichotomy, this schizophrenia has prevailed over humanity for thousands of years.

He says, "God is love," but still God manages a hell. If God is love, the first thing to be destroyed should be hell; hell should be immediately burned, removed. The very idea of hell is of a very jealous God. But Jesus was born a Jew, lived a Jew, died a Jew; he was not a Christian, he had never heard the word *Christian*. And the Jewish idea of God is not a very beautiful idea.

The Talmud says – the declaration is made in God's own words – "I am a jealous God, very jealous. I am not nice! I am not your uncle!" This God is bound to create hell. In fact, to live even in heaven with such a God who is not your uncle, who is not nice, who is jealous, will be hell. What kind of paradise will you attain by living with him? There will be a despotic, dictatorial atmosphere – no freedom, no love. Jealousy and love cannot exist together.

Even the so-called good people have been the cause of human misery. It hurts because we have never pondered over these things. We have never tried to excavate our past, and all the root causes of our misery are in our past. Remember perfectly well – your past is more dominated by Jesus, Mahavira, Confucius, Krishna, Rama, Buddha than by Alexander the Great, Julius Caesar, Tamerlane, Genghis Khan, Nadir Shah. History books talk about these people, but they are not part of your unconscious. They may be part of history, but they don't make up your personality; your personality is made by so-called good people. Certainly, they had a few good qualities in them, but side by side there was a duality, and the duality arose from the idea of perfection.

Jainas say that Mahavira never perspired. How can a perfect man perspire? I can perspire – I am not a perfect man! Perspiration in summer is so beautiful that I would rather choose perspiration than perfection! A man who does not perspire simply has a plastic body, synthetic, nonbreathing, nonporous. The whole body breathes, that's why you perspire; perspiration is a natural process to keep your body temperature constantly the same. Now, Mahavira must be burning inside like hell! How will he manage to keep his body temperature constant? Without perspiration it cannot be done, it is impossible.

Jainas say that when a snake wounded Mahavira's feet, milk, not blood, flowed out of the feet. Now, milk is possible only if Mahavira's feet were not feet but breasts, and a man who has breasts on his feet should be put in a circus! This is their idea of perfection: a perfect man cannot have a dirty thing like blood, he is full of milk and honey. But just imagine: a man full of milk and honey will stink! Milk will turn into curd, and the honey will attract all kinds of mosquitoes and flies; he will be completely covered with flies! I don't like this kind of perfection.

Mahavira is so perfect that he does not urinate, does not defecate; these things are for imperfect human beings. You cannot imagine Mahavira sitting on a toilet seat, impossible! But then where does all his shit disappear to? He must be the shittiest man in the world.

I have read in medical journals about a man – this was the longest case of constipation: eighteen months. These medical people are not aware of Mahavira. He lasted *forty* years! This is the longest period that any man has been able to control his bowels. This is real yoga! The greatest case of constipation in the whole history of man...and I don't think anybody is going to defeat him.

These stupid ideas have been perpetuated just to make humanity suffer. If you have these ideas in your mind then you will feel guilty about everything. Pissing, you are guilty – what are you doing? Sitting on a toilet, and you are falling into hell! If you bleed, a deep humiliation.

Jesus walks on water; he tries to revive a dead friend, but cannot survive, himself, on the cross. He tries to cure blind people, deaf people, but cannot make a single stupid man enlightened, cannot help a single fool to come out of his foolishness, cannot save a single human being by hitting him hard on the head and saying, "See, the goose is out!"

Yes, I am very fallible because I am not a neurotic, I am not psychotic; I am not a perfectionist. I love my imperfections...I love this world because it is imperfect. It *is* imperfect, and that's why it is growing; if it were perfect it would be dead. Growth is possible only if there is imperfection. Perfection means a full stop; perfection means ultimate death; there is no way to go beyond it.

I would like you to remember again and again: I am imperfect, the whole universe is imperfect, and to love this imperfection, to rejoice in this imperfection is my whole message.

The psychiatrist leaned back and placed the tips of his fingers together while he soothed the deeply-troubled man who stood before him. "Calm yourself, my good fellow," he gently urged. "I have helped a great many others with fixations far more serious than yours. Now, let me see if I understand the problem correctly. You indicate that in moments of great emotional stress you believe that you are a dog, a fox terrier. Is that not so?"

"Yes, sir," mumbled the patient. "A small fox terrier with black and brown spots. Oh, please tell me you can help me, doctor. If this keeps up much longer, I don't know what I'll do..."

The doctor gestured toward the couch. "Now, now," he soothed, "the first thing to do is lie down here, and we'll see if we can't get to the root of your delusion."

"Oh, I couldn't do that, doctor," said the patient. "I'm not allowed up on the furniture."

Once you get an idea deep-rooted in you, it starts becoming a reality. Perfectionism is a neurotic idea. Infallibility is good for stupid Polack popes but not for intelligent people. An intelligent person will understand that life is an adventure, a constant exploration through trial and error. That's its very joy, its very juice!

I don't want you to be perfect. I want you to be just as perfectly imperfect as possible. Rejoice in your imperfections! Rejoice in your very ordinariness! Beware of so-called "His Holinesses" – they are all "His Phoninesses." If you like such big words like "His Holiness" then make a title such as "His Very Ordinariness" – HVO, not HH! I preach ordinariness. I make no claims for any miracles; I am a simple man. I would like you to be very simple also so that you can get rid of these two polarities: one of guilt and the other of hypocrisy. Exactly in the middle is sanity.

St. Peter challenged the Archangel Gabriel to a game of golf. St. Peter's first drive resulted in a hole-in-one. Gabriel's first drive produced the same result. The same thing happened at the next shot.

St. Peter looked at Gabriel thoughtfully and then said, "What do you say we cut out the miracles and play some golf?"

I am not infallible, and I would never like to be infallible either, because that is suicidal. I would like to commit as many mistakes as possible and I would like to go on committing mistakes to the very end of my last breath, because that means life. If you are capable of committing mistakes even to the very last breath you have conquered death.

A Zen Master was dying.... I have a deep love for the Zen approach for the simple reason that they also rejoice in ordinariness. That's the beauty of Zen: no religion has been able to rise to such heights of ordinariness.

The Master was very old, around eighty years of age. He gathered his disciples and said, "Now this is my last day. I don't think I will be able to see the sunset, and the sun is setting on the horizon. I have called you all to suggest to me some new way to die."

They were a little puzzled. They said, "What do you mean by 'new way'?"

He said, "People have died in bed, people have died in the bathroom, people have died this way and that. All those things have been done before, and I always like to do things in a new way, in my own way. Can you suggest something? Have you ever heard of somebody dying in a standing posture?"

There was silence. One man said, "Yes, I have heard about a Zen Master who died standing."

He said, "Then that is dropped! Have you heard of anybody dying standing upside-down, on his head, doing a *sirshasana*, a headstand?"

Everybody said, "We have not heard of such a thing. We have not even imagined such a thing, that anybody would die standing on his head!"

So he said, "That will do!" The old man stood on his head, and it is said that there were all the visible signs that he was dead. But there was a difficulty: the difficulty was that the Zen disciples were in a very puzzling situation; what were they to do with this old man now? They had never heard of any ritual for somebody dying standing on his head. What should be done? They knew perfectly well what had to be done when somebody died in bed, but what should they do with this man? He was standing there dead – on his head!

Somebody suggested: "We should run... His old sister lives very close by; she is a nun. She may be able to do something or suggest something. She is even crazier than this old man!"

So they ran to the sister. She came and shouted at her brother and said, "Look, your whole life you have been a trouble! At least die peacefully; don't make much fuss about it! Why are you driving these poor disciples crazy? Get up and lie down on the bed!"

The old man laughed, got up and lay down on the bed, and he asked, "Who has brought this crazy sister of mine here? She won't even let me die in an improper way!"

Then he said, "Okay, you can be happy. This is your last desire, and I have never followed any advice of yours. At least this much I can do before I depart."

However, the woman did not stand there to see him depart. She said, "You just lie down there; I am going. You die on the bed in a proper way! No more trouble."

And she left, and the old man died in the bed in a proper way.

This is how life should be lived.

I am not a saint; I am not a sage. All those hocus-pocus words don't mean anything to me. I am certainly a little bit crazy, and it is because of my craziness that you can rely on me! Never rely on saints, never rely on sages – they will drive you nuts!

It was teatime in the pad, and the air hung heavy in thick blue folds as the bunch of Beatniks and their tourist friends lit up. Suddenly, a loud voice in the hall demanded that they open the door in the name of the law. The smokers frantically gathered their still-smoking weed and stuffed it in the cuckoo clock. The police entered, searched diligently, found nothing and left. The bunch breathed a sigh of relief and made for the cuckoo clock just as the clock's hands announced 3 a.m. The little door popped open, the bird poked his head out and said, "Hey, man, what time is it?"

The second question:

Osho,
I have heard that behind each so-called great man – like Julius Caesar or Napoleon, or even a really great man like Socrates – there was a woman in charge.
I have always managed to turn from being an admirer of women into a woman's fool. What is your secret?
You have put more women in charge than is really possible, and yet you have remained free and loved by them all. And I love you too.

The so-called great men – Julius Caesar, Alexander, Napoleon and others – were certainly driven by women; they were trying to prove themselves.

Woman has one very special quality about her: she is, in a way, very contented with small things. Just because she is a woman she has a natural capacity to create children; her desire for creativity is fulfilled – she becomes a creator naturally, biologically. There, man feels impotent: he cannot produce children. Something like an empty womb hurts inside. He wants to prove before the woman, particularly the woman he loves, that "I can also create," that "I can also conquer," that "I can also show the world that I am not just useless, just like an appendix," that "I have also something to contribute to the world, to its beauty, to its power, to its art, to its music, to its dance. I have to prove it!"

That is a very unconscious longing in every man – to prove something. The moment a man falls in love with a woman, immediately the question becomes of predominant importance. He starts proving himself by earning more money, by becoming a president or prime minister, by conquering the world. Whatsoever he does still remains incomplete – he cannot compete with the woman. She remains so round, so centered and grounded, that the man can go on to the very end of the world, but still he will not be grounded. He will go to Everest, he will go to the moon, he will become a world conqueror, he will discover great truths of science, he will fight wars, he will explore the unknown, but wherever he is he will find that something is missing. That missing link is biological.

Woman has a balanced biology; her chemistry is equally balanced. Man has a biology which is a little unbalanced: one part is heavier and the other part is a little lighter, and that creates an inner tension in him. That's why more men go mad than women, more men commit suicide than women, more men commit murder than women. And if you look at the world you will see that it is dominated by man for the simple reason that woman is not interested in dominating; there is no need – she feels a certain kind of fulfillment in her innermost core. Man is always rushing, going somewhere, always on the go. All men are American tourists! They cannot be here, now.

It starts even in the womb. An experienced mother who has given birth to one or two children knows perfectly well after a few months whether inside the womb there is a boy or a girl. The boy starts kicking, he starts becoming an Alexander the Great! The girl remains quiet, at ease, meditative; she does not create much disturbance.

It is because of this that woman was easily dominated by man. It is not because of the superiority of man. It is not because of his power, that he was able to dominate the woman; it is just the opposite. Woman is superior in many ways, and because man suffers from inferiority he has to dominate the woman; only then can he get rid of a little bit of his inferiority.

Man has dominated the whole of history; he has in every possible way tried to enslave woman, but he has not been successful. On the surface it may look as if he has succeeded, but each husband knows perfectly well that the moment he enters the home he is no longer the lion that he pretends to be on the outside. He suddenly becomes a dog, a poor dog, with its tail between its legs! When he goes out of the home he goes like thunder, when he comes home all the gas is lost! Somehow he enters afraid, trembling, and starts reading the same newspaper he has been reading the whole day just to avoid his woman. That newspaper is just a curtain. Even a small woman is enough to bring any Muhammad Ali the Great to his senses.

There is a beautiful story in the life of the great Indian Emperor Akbar:

One day one of his friends, Birbal, told him, "As far as I know, all men are dominated by women, whatsoever they may pretend." Akbar was offended. He said, "You will have to prove it. There must be a few men who are not dominated; your statement cannot be taken as a generalization. So I will give you two beautiful horses. You go around, and take a few hens also with you. If you find a man who is henpecked, present him with a hen. If you find a man who is not henpecked, then give him a choice: he can either have the black horse or the white horse. These are the most beautiful horses I have got, the most costly." In those days horses were of tremendous value.

Birbal went around Delhi, and wherever he went he had to present a hen. Only in one place was he in a little difficulty. A very muscular man – he had never seen such a strong, muscular body – was sitting in the sun, massaging his muscles.

Birbal asked him, "Are you a henpecked husband?"

He simply showed his muscles to Birbal and said, "Just hold my hand and I will show you!" He crushed Birbal's hand so that Birbal screamed, and he said, "Now, do you have to ask me again? Then I will hit you! The very question is an insult! Who can dominate me?"

A very little woman was cooking food inside – just a little woman that the man could have crushed with a single hand. No cross would have been needed, just a little pressure on her neck and she would have kicked the bucket!

Birbal asked, "Where is your wife?"

He said, "That is my wife cooking inside. You can look at her and you can look at me, and you can decide who is the master."

It was so absolutely clear that Birbal said, "Certainly you are the master, so I will have to take my generalization back. You can choose as a gift from the king either of the horses, black or white."

And the man looked at the woman and said, "Which horse should I choose, black or white?"

And the woman said, "Make it the white one!"

Birbal said, "Now you get a hen! It is finished! You may have muscular power, but that does not prove anything."

The woman has a psychological grip.

Andrew Carnegie, one of the great wealthy industrialists of the world, was asked on the last day of his life, "How did you manage to earn so much money? What was the secret behind it?"

He said, "There was no secret. I was just trying to see whether I can earn so much that my wife could not spend it, but I failed, she succeeded."

You ask me: "I have heard that behind each so-called great man – like Julius Caesar or Napoleon, or even a really great man like Socrates – there was a woman in charge."

It is true. About the so-called great men it is true because they were trying to be great just to compete with their wives, and about the really great men like Socrates it is also true.

A young man asked Socrates, "I am thinking to get married. What is your advice?"

He had heard all the stories about Socrates and his wife, Xanthippe. She must have been a really dangerous woman, an Amazon! She used to beat Socrates. Once she poured hot water, boiling hot water on him; she was preparing it for tea but became angry and poured it on Socrates' face.

Socrates was an ugly man, very ugly – snub-nosed, nothing worth looking at, disgusting. Xanthippe made him more disgusting! Half of his face remained burned his whole life.

So this young man had come to the right person to ask, "You have experienced what it is to be a husband more than anybody else, and the whole of Athens is full of stories about your wife and you, and you are the wisest man, declared so by the Oracle of Delphi, so I have

come to ask you – I am in a dilemma – should I get married or not?"
Socrates said, "You should get married."
The young man could not believe it! He had not expected this
answer. He said, "You are saying it after your whole experience of
having Xanthippe as your wife?"
He said, "Yes. If you get a good wife she will make you succeed
in life, she will put ambitions in you. You are young; you will need
some ambitions. If you get a wife like mine then you will become a
philosopher. My wife has helped me immensely to learn the art of
remaining unaffected. Whatsoever happens – success or failure,
misery or happiness – it is all the same to me. She has made me
centered. Either way you will not lose, so get married."

There is a possibility – every possibility, in fact – that the whole
credit for Buddha becoming enlightened goes to Yashodhara, his
wife. The whole credit for Mohammed becoming the prophet of God
must go to his nine wives. There is every possibility that these people
were trying somehow not to be disturbed, not to be distracted, and
they started searching for a beyond, they started searching for a
within, the beyond within, so that they could forget the whole world.
A wife, your woman, is really the closest world around you: she
surrounds you from everywhere, from every nook and corner. Your
so-called great men are indebted to women, and your many really
great men are also indebted to women, although they have not
accepted it. That is ugly.
Many times I am asked why women don't become enlightened.
The reason is, no man is capable of driving them to that extreme! It
has nothing to do with women, it is just the impotence of the man –
he cannot drive them to that point. Moreover, women are always
grounded, centered; man is not grounded, not centered. He remains
airy-fairy and he needs grounding, he needs centering.

Strolling through London's Soho district, the young Cockney
noticed an attractive girl furiously struggling to hold down her
microskirt in the brisk wind. Tipping his hat, he said, "Airy, ain't it?"
"What the hell did you expect?" she replied. "Feathers?"

Sheila and George were spending the first night of their honeymoon in a quaint medieval town in France. To add piquancy to the

evening, Sheila suggested coyly that they make love every time the old night watchman rang his hourly bell. George smiled in delight at this prospect, but four rings later he pretended that he had to go out to get some cigarettes and staggered off to the watchman's tower.

"Listen, old man," he wheezed to that worthy man, "do me a favor, will you? For the rest of the night ring that bell of yours at two-hour intervals instead of hourly!"

"Ah," replied the ancient watchman, fingering his mustache, "I would be happy to oblige, monsieur, but I cannot do this."

"Why not?" George demanded. "I'll give you money, if that's what's troubling you!"

"Not at all," the old man responded. "You see, a beautiful young lady has already bribed me to ring the bell every half hour."

"I have always managed to turn from being an admirer of women into a woman's fool..." If you are an admirer of women you will inevitably turn into a woman's fool, because admiration is illusory; admiration is possible only from a distance. The closer you come the more foolish you will look, and when you are caught by the woman you are bound to be turned into a damned fool. You were trying in every possible way to be caught, so you cannot easily get out of it.

A mousetrap never runs after a mouse; the mousetrap simply sits centered, grounded. The mouse in his airy-fairy romanticism starts dreaming about the coziness inside the mousetrap, the smell of the food inside, the spaghetti and all that, and gets caught. It is easy to get caught, it is very difficult to get out again, because the mousetrap has only an entrance and no exit.

So, it is going to happen again and again!

I don't admire any woman: I am not a romantic, I am very factual. Whatsoever I say about men or women is simply a fact – no fiction about it! And once you are caught you will be constantly in difficulty because there are other mousetraps all around which look cozier, warmer, more beautiful, more spicy. In fact, the word *spicy* is only a plural of *spouse*! Marriage is a very strange affair: the dessert is served first and then everything goes down the drain!

After a heart-transplant operation the patient was receiving instructions from his doctor. He was placed on a strict diet, denied tobacco and advised to get at least eight hours sleep at night.

Finally the patient asked, "What about my sex life, Doc? Will it be all right for me to have intercourse?"

"Just with your wife," responded the doctor. "We don't want you to get too excited."

A middle-aged husband went to a doctor and explained that his wife was constantly nagging him about his vanishing potency. After giving him a bottle of pills the doctor assured him that they would work wonders.

A month later the man returned, obviously satisfied with the results. "The pills are terrific!" he said. "I have been doing it three times a night."

"Wonderful," the doctor replied. "What does your wife say about your lovemaking now?"

"How should I know?" the fellow shrugged. "I have not been home yet!"

You ask me: "What is your secret?"

In my life there is no secret – or you can call it "the open secret." I have nothing hidden; I don't live like a fist, I live like an open hand. Nothing is hidden, nothing is esoteric, nothing is secret; all is simple and plain.

You say: "You have put more women in charge than is really possible, and yet you have remained free and loved by them all."

The open secret is that you can be free only if you have put too many women around you. Then they are so concerned with each other that they leave you absolutely alone. In fact, they forget all about you! Their jealousies, their envies are enough to keep them occupied. If one wants to be really free of women, that's the only way. This is my open secret!

They all love me for the simple reason that I am not possessed by anybody, nor do I possess anybody. If you possess some woman then there will be trouble; if you are possessed by some woman then there will be trouble. I don't possess anybody; I am not possessed by anybody. I go on sitting, doing my own business – which is nothing – and I keep the women going round and round. They have so many problems; they can afford to forget all about me!

You say, "You have put more women in charge than is really possible..." No, you don't know the limit. Even the sky is not the limit! When the new commune happens you will see: I will put so many women in charge that even if I die it will take you years to discover that a man is no longer there! They will make so much fuss and dance and love and all kinds of foolish things that you will not even come to know whether I am still here or gone.

I have put them in charge because they are more pragmatic than men, they have a greater capacity to cope with reality, they are earthbound. Man leans more toward the sky and woman is rooted in the earth. It is a very pragmatic arrangement.

If women take charge of the whole world, the world will drop many stupid things. For example, wars will disappear. Of course, there will be more beautiful clothes, fashion shows, modeling; but weapons, atomic bombs, hydrogen bombs, etcetera, will disappear. No woman is interested in all these things. Hiroshima and Nagasaki will not happen again; it is only man who can do these things. Crusades will disappear, religious wars will disappear, jihads will disappear. No woman is interested; her interest is very pragmatic, real. She is more interested in clothes, in cosmetics, in beauty; and those concerns are good – they keep you more alive. Man's concerns are very dangerous – political, religious, economic – and they make more and more mischief.

In the name of serving humanity more mischief happens than anything else: in three thousand years, five thousand wars have been fought and the whole credit goes to men. Millions of people are killed in the name of love, in the name of democracy, in the name of freedom, in the name of God. Now, no woman can do that. I don't think you can have a world war because of cosmetics, or clothes and designs, or dramas and new dishes – you can't have world wars because of these things!

I want my commune to be very earthbound, because this is my experience, the observation of many lives: that the tree has first to go deep into the earth; the deeper the roots go, the higher the branches rise. If you want to touch the stars with the flowers then you have to go to the very rock bottom of the earth.

All the religions of the world have remained a little foggy, confused, for the simple reason that they were all trying to reach the stars, the beyond, to the far away, without ever thinking about the roots.

Buddha was against women; he was not willing to initiate women. He said that his religion would have lasted five thousand years, but because he finally agreed to initiate women his religion would disappear within five hundred years. My own observation is just the opposite: without women it would not have lasted even five hundred years, because the moment Buddha died all the men started quarreling – ideological wars. Thirty-two sects were immediately born, the same day! Buddha's body was not yet even totally burned and thirty-two philosophical schools, thirty-two interpretations arose. The war had started.

When Jesus was crucified, all those twelve fools disappeared. Three women were there to take his body from the cross, but not a single man. Mary Magdalene was there, the prostitute, her sister was there, Martha, and Jesus' mother Mary was there. All those apostles, those fanatics, where had they gone? They were preparing for the Vatican, they were preparing for the future. Jesus was finished! Now the question was of theology, philosophy, ideology. Those three women were not concerned with theology or philosophy, they were concerned with his body. They were more pragmatic; they were more true, honest, sincere. They loved the man, they risked for the man, they were ready to be condemned. All those men had disappeared.

One of the most educated of Jesus' disciples was Judas; he betrayed him for only thirty silver coins. No woman could have done that. He was the most intellectual among all of Jesus' disciples. But intellectuals can betray very easily: they are the most renegade people in the world because their hearts are not in it, only their heads – and the head is cunning, the head is calculating. Woman lives through the heart.

Hence, my commune is functioning in a totally new way: it has to be rooted first. That's the way of all gardeners: first you have to give soil, manure, roots to the plant, and then flowers come of their own accord. Flowers will come, but they cannot come without roots. Roots and flowers are like two wings: if you have both wings then the whole sky is yours. But the most important thing, the first, the basic, the fundamental, is the roots.

Woman is the root of all life; man can at the most be a branch, a flowering branch, a beautiful branch – a longing, an aspiration to touch the stars. They have to go together. That's why I have put so many women here, and slowly, slowly they will take over the whole soil and leave you free, leave men free to grow into flowers.

A real commune will have men and women in a deep

synchronicity. All the past communes had to die because they depended only on men; they never took any care of the women. No woman has ever been able to create a commune because she does not aspire to the stars.

A commune means an aspiration, a longing, a tremendous longing to grow, an immense urge to explore. No woman can find reasons to put down the foundation stone for a commune. Man is always interested in the far away, so he becomes the original source of communes, but no man is capable of giving roots.

This has been the problem in the past: woman can provide roots but she is not interested in flowers, and man can provide flowers but he is not interested in roots. A deep synchronicity is needed, a deep harmony. That's what I am trying to fulfill here.

Obsessed with the idea of pleasing all manner of customers with girls of the very highest order, an enterprising madam set up a three-story house of sport. She had ex-secretaries, selected for their efficiency, on the first floor; ex-models, selected for their beauty, on the second; and ex-schoolteachers, selected for their intelligence, on the third. As time went on the madam noticed that almost all the play went to floor number three. She asked why, and the answer to the puzzle finally came from one of the steady customers.

"Well," said the sporting gentleman, "you know how those school teachers are. They make you do it over and over, until you get it right!"

This is really the open secret: my women sannyasins are really doing perfectly well, and they will make you do it again and again until you do it right!

The morning after the office Christmas party the husband woke up with an agonizing hangover. "I feel terrible," he complained.

"You should," said his wife. "You really made a fool of yourself last night."

"What did I do?"

"You got into a quarrel with your boss and he fired you."

"Well, he can go to hell!"

"That's exactly what you told him."

"I did?" he said incredulously. "Then, screw the old goat!"

"That's just what I did," his wife replied. "You go back to work on Monday."

Very pragmatic!

Sam told his wife, Becky, that because of inflation they had to cut expenses – no more dining out, theater, concerts, etcetera. Becky chided him in reply, "But, Sam, if you would just learn how to fuck, we could get rid of the chauffeur!"

Man lives in a totally different world!

A man returned from a convention and proudly showed his wife a gallon of bourbon he had won for having the largest sex organ of all present.

"What!" she exclaimed. "Do you mean to tell me you exhibited yourself in front of all those people?"

"Only enough to win, darling," he replied. "Only enough to win!"

The third question:

Osho,
I have begun to ask you some questions three or four times already. Every time I finished a letter, I felt that everything I wrote was nonsense and so I threw them into the wastepaper basket. Nevertheless, I want you to speak a few words to me, although I seldom listen to your words – just hearing, just being close to you. Since I arrived here I have been really irritated. I was fine in the West and have never searched for a master. Now I am here and have no desire to go back. What has happened to me?

I have happened to you! Now there is no going back, and even if you go I am coming with you. I will haunt you everywhere! I can understand your irritation. That's my whole joy – to irritate people! Once they are irritated they are caught.

Of course, you are right that you were fine in the West; now you can never be fine anywhere else, but only now, here. Now no West, no East can be of any help. You have tasted something that you have not tasted before, and once you have tasted something – something alcoholic, something like LSD – you can never be the same person again. That taste will linger; it will haunt you.

And this is pure LSD that is happening here! It is not chemical LSD, it is alchemical – far more refined than chemical LSDs can ever be. It is real soma! It is what has always happened between a master and a disciple.

There is no need to listen to my words. Just being with me is enough, just being in tune, that's enough. Words are only strategies to keep you attuned to me so that you don't fall asleep, so that you remain awake.

You say: "Every time I finished a letter, I felt that everything I wrote was nonsense..." It is! But there is no need to throw it away, otherwise what am I going to do here? Use me as a wastepaper basket, so whatsoever you write – sense, nonsense...it is *all* non-sense; as far as I am concerned it is all nonsense. So you can send it to me, and I will make some crazy thing out of it.

After acquiring enough money from handouts, an inhabitant of the Bowery decided to take his refreshment at one of Wall Street's better drinking establishments.

A financial tycoon seated next to him was visibly appalled at the appearance and odor of the down-and-outer, so much so, in fact, that he turned to the man and pointedly said, "Cleanliness is next to godliness – John Wesley." His words were ignored.

A few minutes later, the financier again intoned loudly, "Clean-liness is next to godliness – John Wesley." Still he was ignored.

Finally, the visibly irritated financier shouted in the man's face, "Cleanliness is next to godliness – John Wesley!"

To which the skid-row denizen calmly replied, "Screw you! – Tennessee Williams."

You can ask me any nonsense thing, and I will give you a bigger nonsense. I am an expert at that – the only expertise I can claim! And the more nonsensical a question is the more I enjoy it, because it expects a more nonsensical answer. If you ask something crazy that means you are asking *for* something crazy, and I am the last one to be defeated!

A man went into a restaurant and ordered his breakfast. When the waitress brought his coffee, he observed that her thumb was stuck in the coffee. When the scrambled eggs arrived, again he observed that her thumb was in the eggs.

This was too much, and he said, "Lady, I didn't say anything when I saw your thumb in my coffee, but now I see that your thumb is in my eggs, too."

"Well," said the waitress, "I have a painful arthritis in my thumb joint, and the doctor told me to put it into something warm and this would ease the pain."

The man was angry and said, "Well, why don't you stick it up your ass?"

"Oh, I do, I do," answered the waitress, "but only when I'm in the kitchen!"

Enough for today.

i exalt the ordinary

The first question:

Osho,
I have got all the degrees that a university can offer. Why am I still
ignorant?

K nowledge has no capacity to dispel ignorance. Knowledge is a
false phenomenon; it is not wisdom at all, it is just the opposite of wisdom.

Knowledge is borrowed; wisdom is the flowering of your innermost being. You can borrow a plastic flower, but if you want real
roses then you will have to grow them in your innermost being. No
university can offer it, no scripture can offer it, no scholarship is
capable of doing it. They are all impotent efforts, but they have been
deceiving millions of people for thousands of years. Yes, they can
make you knowledgeable. To be knowledgeable is one thing, and to
know is totally different.

A blind man can be knowledgeable about light, but he knows
nothing of light; he has not experienced it. He can collect all kinds of
information about light, he can argue, philosophize, systematize; he

can write great treatises on light, but he has not tasted the joy of light – he has not seen even a single ray of light. He has not seen the rainbow, the colors of the flowers, the wings of a butterfly. He has not seen the green trees, he has not seen the stars, the sun, the moon. He has missed all that. And what he has accumulated is simply rubbish.

It is better to be ignorant and have eyes than to be very knowledgeable about light and be blind.

The universities exist for that purpose specifically. No society wants you to become wise – it is against the investment of all societies. If people are wise they cannot be exploited. If they are intelligent they cannot be subjugated; they cannot be forced into a mechanical life, to live like a robot. They will assert themselves – they will assert their individuality. They will have the fragrance of rebellion around them; they would like to live in freedom.

Freedom comes with wisdom, intrinsically – they are inseparable – and no society wants people to be free. The communist society, the fascist society, the capitalist society, the Hindu, the Mohammedan, the Christian – no society would like people to use their own intelligence because the moment they start using their intelligence they become dangerous, dangerous to the establishment, dangerous to the people who are in power, dangerous to the "haves," dangerous to all kinds of oppression, exploitation, suppression; dangerous to the churches, dangerous to the states, dangerous to the nations.

In fact, a wise man is afire, alive, aflame. He would prefer to die than to be enslaved. Death will not matter much, but he cannot sell his life to any kind of stupidity, to any kind of stupid people. He cannot serve them. Hence, societies down the ages have been supplying you with false knowing. That's the very function of your schools, colleges, universities.

They don't serve *you*. Remember, they serve the past, they serve the vested interests. Of course, they go on puffing your ego up bigger and bigger, they go on giving you more and more degrees. Your name becomes longer and longer. But just the name – you go on becoming shorter and shorter. A point comes where there are only certificates, and the man has disappeared. First the man carries the certificates, then the certificates carry the man. The man is long dead.

It is not possible to become wise through the universities. Wisdom needs a totally different approach, a diametrically opposite approach. Knowledge is of the mind; wisdom is a state of no-mind. Knowledge creates the bottle around the goose – a beautiful bottle, very beautifully painted, but it is just a bottle.

Inside there cannot be a real goose, alive. Inside a bottle either you can have a stuffed goose – that's what your scholars are, stuffed tomatoes, potatoes, but all stuffed, stuffed with junk – or you can have a painted goose inside. It will look beautiful from the outside, but in fact you are carrying only a bottle.

The bottle becomes heavier, because knowledge has its own way of accumulating; it goes on reproducing itself. Knowledge does not believe in birth control at all. If you know one thing, it will drive you into another, because as each question is answered ten new questions arise. Again the same will happen: ten questions are answered and you have a hundred questions ready for you. It goes on spreading. It becomes bigger and bigger and you are lost in it.

You ask me: "Why I am still ignorant?"

This is why you are ignorant: you have not yet come out of the illusion of knowledge, the illusion of the mind.

Get out of the mind. The mind is the bottle I am talking about. The moment you drop the mind...and mind is only your idea; it is not a reality, it is fictitious, it is just a fantasy. It is made of the same stuff as dreams are made of. You can simply step out of it.

This is the moment, because this is a great insight, in fact, to recognize this: "Why am I still ignorant when I am carrying all the degrees of the university?" Accept the fact that all those years of acquiring knowledge have been a sheer wastage. Get out of it! The moment you are out of the mind, you are out of the bottle. See... the goose is out! And the whole freedom of the sky, and the whole freedom of insightfulness...

Just the other day I was reading:

What does a degree mean? I have got four: B.A., M.A., Ph.D., and LL.D. Put them all together and what have you got? – BAMAPHDLLD!

A young man at college named Breeze,
Weighed down by M.A.s and LL.Ds
Collapsed from the strain.
Said his doctor, "'Tis plain,
You are killing yourself by degrees!"

A very agitated professor, a father-to-be, desperate for a son, was pacing up and down in the waiting room at the maternity hospital. Eventually the midwife came out of the delivery room and said to him, "It's all over, Dr. Jones. Congratulations!"

Still in a state of total panic he replied, "Am I a father or a mother?"

That's what it means: BAMAPHDLLD.

A professor-couple living in the country received an invitation from the local squire to a costume party. They decided to go as a cow, with the husband at the front and the wife at the back.

The party was to be held in the squire's mansion, which was only across a couple of fields, so they thought they might as well walk across in costume.

They had only gotten half way across the field when the husband, in the front, said to his wife, "Don't panic, darling, but there is a bull looking at us."

So they kept walking and the bull kept looking. Then the bull started pawing the ground and making his way toward them in a meaningful manner.

"He's charging us, darling, he's charging!" said the husband.

"What are we going to do?" yelled the wife.

So the husband said, "I am going to bend down and eat grass – you had better brace yourself!"

It was the young British professor's first visit to the United States, and in his innocence he sought lodging in the city's red-light district. His money, however, was as green as his outlook, and the madam gladly offered him a room for the night.

When a friend questioned him about his accommodation over lunch the following day, the young Briton replied, "Well, the room was very pretentious, you know, but Gad! what maid service!"

The so-called learned, the scholarly, the knowledgeable go on living in a world of their own fictions. They have no concern with reality at all; they are disconnected from the real. And it is the real which can make your life a joy, a bliss.

The word *God* is not God, the word *love* is not love either. So the poor people who go on thinking about the word *God* or the word *love* are simply missing a great opportunity. They may have known what God is, they may have become acquainted with the mysteries of love, but the word is hiding the truth; the word is covering their eyes. All the eyes of the knowledgeable people are so covered with theories, theologies, dogmas, creeds, that they cannot see. They are not transparent. And wisdom is a transparency, a vision unclouded – unclouded by all thoughts, unclouded by all dust.

One has to cleanse oneself every moment, because dust tends to gather on the mirror every moment. It is a natural process. While you are sitting here, the mirror in your bathroom is gathering dust. Even in the night when nothing is happening – even when the doors of the bathroom and the windows are closed – still some dust is gathering, settling on the mirror, because dust particles are there in the air itself. In the morning you have to cleanse the mirror every day.

One has to be even more alert about the inner mind, the inner mirror, the inner capacity for reflection. *Each* moment you have to cleanse the dust. I prefer to put it in this way: *each* moment a sannyasin has to die to the past and be born anew. Then he remains transparent, then his mirror remains clear. Then there is nothing to obstruct his perspective. Then he is not a Christian, nor a Hindu, nor a Mohammedan, nor a Buddhist. Then he is simply a mirror, just a mirror, a mirroring – mirroring all that is, within and without. Out of that mirroring, wisdom is born.

Wisdom is the flowering of your transparency, of your translucency, of your luminous being. That's what we are doing here. In fact, the function of the master is to undo what the society has done to you. It is an anti-university, anti-school, anti-college, because it is not to impart knowledge to you but to impart something totally different, something of a different dimension. It is to create a triggering process in you so that you can get out of your so-called scriptures, words, theories, and you can become just ordinary. You can just become whatsoever you are without any pretensions.

I exalt the ordinariness of consciousness. I am not teaching here you as the superman. Friedrich Nietzsche went mad simply because of the idea of the superman. In India also, Sri Aurobindo, his whole life, was feeding the Indian ego with the idea of the superman, of the supermind, of the supernatural.

All this esoteric nonsense has become such a heavy burden on man that it has to be totally burned – less than that won't do. A fire is needed so all that can be burned can be burned, and only that which remains after will be your true self.

I am not esoteric, I am not occult, I am not teaching you the other world, I am not teaching you the supernatural, the superman. I am simply exalting the very ordinariness of every human being, the very ordinariness not only of human beings, but of animals, of trees, of rivers, and rocks – this very ordinariness is godliness. To me, godliness and ordinariness are equivalent, synonymous.

If I have to choose I will drop the word *God*, because it has become really god-damned. Just pure ordinariness...and to live it moment-to-moment, joyously, dancingly, celebratingly. Then wisdom blooms. Then the spring comes and the grass grows by itself.

The second question:

Osho,
Your compassion toward India brings, in return, anger and condemnation toward you. Every day Indian newspapers and magazines are full of third-rate criticism against you. Even so, you keep hammering this rotten culture. What is this business? Does India deserve so much compassion?

It is because I am saying something which India has completely forgotten. It hurts. It has forgotten the truth. For thousands of years it has lived in a foggy state of mind – not only that, it has become very attached to that foggy state for the simple reason that it has nothing else to cling to. This was the only prop for its ego.

For twenty-two centuries India has been in political slavery. Now, a country existing for twenty-two centuries in slavery cannot have any source of ego as far as the political world is concerned. It cannot brag about world conquerors like Alexander the Great.

For five thousand years, India has been living in a very superstitious way. The priests have dominated India more than any country ever, and they are the most cunning people in the world. Because of their exploitation, oppression, because of their poisoning of the Indian soul, for five thousand years India has not been able to find any way into truth. They were standing like a China Wall against the truth.

It is a question of life and death for the priesthood. Either the truth or the priest – both cannot survive together; there is no possibility of their co-existence. If truth wins, the priest disappears. Hence, the truth has not to be allowed to win so the priest can go on dominating. No other country has been dominated by priests like India. For five thousand years a spiritual slavery...

There is nothing to support the ego of the nation – no science, no technology, no richness, no political freedom, no democracy. You can see the problem. The problem is... A nation has to depend on some props, because a nation is not a true reality, remember; it needs props.

The individual can exist without the ego because an individual is a reality and that reality has no need of the ego. But the nation, the race, the church, the state – these cannot exist without egos. Without an ego they will fall apart. It is the ego that functions as a false center and keeps them together. Hence, a Buddha can exist without the ego but Buddhists cannot exist. Krishna can exist without an ego but Hindus cannot exist. Remember this always: a false entity needs a false center, otherwise it will wither away.

India as a country, as a nation, as a race, was in tremendous need somehow to create a false center. There was no ordinary alternative available – money, technology, science, political power – so the only thing to rely on was a spiritual longing, the longing for other world. It is easy, because then you are dealing with invisible goods. Nobody can prove it, nobody can disprove it. It is very easy to live in the hope of the other world. But who will create that hope? Then you have to depend on the crafty priests, the brahmins – they became the mediators. They talk about the other world. They have even given you maps of the other world; they don't know the map of the physical world, this world. If you ask them, "Where is Timbuktu?" they may not be able to answer, but they can tell you each detail of heaven – not only one heaven, but seven heavens, a seven-storied heaven. They can tell you all the details, minute details of seven hells. There is no problem with it; it is religious fiction.

Hindus believe in seven hells. Mahavira believed – Jainas believe in three hells and three heavens. There was a very beautiful man in Mahavira's time – his name was Sanjaya Vilethiputta. He said, "This is all nonsense. There are seven hundred hells and seven hundred heavens!" But people said, "Mahavira says only three, Hindus say only seven." Sanjaya Vilethiputta said, "Because they have only gone that far. I have searched the whole terrain."

Once a follower of Radhaswami came to me. They believe in four-teen heavens, fourteen stages of paradise. Of course, the founder of their religion has reached to the fourteenth. Others are somewhere on the ladder: Rama and Krishna and Buddha are somewhere on the seventh; Jesus, Mohammed and Zarathustra somewhere on the sixth; Nanak, Kabir, Meera, somewhere on the fifth, and so on and so forth…each according to his need, and each according to his capacity…

He had brought the whole map. He wanted my approval – what did I think about this map, what do I say, is it right or not?

I said, "It is absolutely right!"

He was a little shocked because people had told him not to go to me because I will disturb him. And I said, "It is absolutely right. I know. Your guru has reached the fourteenth – I have seen him there."

He said, "What do you mean?"

I said, "I am on the fifteenth, and he is always begging me, 'Pull me out of the fourteenth'!"

He was shocked, he was angry. But if there are fourteen, why not fifteen? Nobody can prove it, nobody can disprove.

I have heard: In New York a shopkeeper was selling invisible hairpins. And, of course, the women were immensely attracted – invisible hairpins!

One woman looked in the box… Of course, when the hairpins are invisible you cannot see – the box looked empty. She said, "Are they really there?"

The shopkeeper said, "They must be! Nobody has ever seen. In fact, for months we have run out of stock, but they are selling!"

When something is invisible you can go on selling it; there is no problem with it.

India has been selling invisible goods to the world. Visible goods are not there. Naturally they become angry with me because I insist that goods should be visible, that you are carrying an empty box, that there is no goose in your bottle. For five thousand years they have been doing such a good business and I am destroying their very foundation.

It is natural that they get angry at me. But anger simply shows fear. Remember always: anger is fear standing on its head. It is always fear that hides behind anger; fear is the other side of anger.

Whenever you become afraid, the only way to hide the fear is to be angry because fear will expose you. Anger will create a curtain around you; you can hide behind anger. The Indian mind is becoming really afraid of me. And it is not only the Indian mind but all other minds in the world who are doing the same kind of business, dealing in invisible goods. They all are becoming afraid.

When they become angry with me I know that I have hit on the right point. I rejoice in it! They have been pretending love, compassion, sympathy, understanding, but I am exposing them to their very core. Without knowing what they are doing, they are doing what *I* want them to do. They are in my hands. Anybody who gets angry at me is caught by me. Now he will be in a whirlwind. I will churn him, I will haunt him. Sooner or later he will himself throw his clothes off and stand naked in the sun. That's what is happening. When they are angry at me they are really showing that they have been exposed.

The only way to defend themselves is to be aggressive. They are defending themselves, but they can defend only if they become aggressive. Their anger is showing simply their impotence.

I have heard a beautiful story, an ancient story:

A man came to China. When he entered the country – this must be an old, ancient story – just on the boundary he saw a crowd. Two persons were almost ready to kill each other. They were shouting, jumping, making all kinds of angry gestures, swords naked in their hands. But nothing real was happening, as if it was a movie, as if it was just a play. The man could not detect any anger on their faces. Their eyes were calm and quiet, their faces were relaxed. They looked very centered and grounded. Why all this shouting and swinging of swords, and jumping and jogging and running at each other? Nobody was being hit, and nobody was preventing them either. The crowd was simply standing there witnessing the whole scene.

The man became a little tired after a while, a little bored too. One needs some excitement, something should happen. And then one of the men became angry; his face became red, his eyes became flaming. And the crowd dispersed! The fight ended there.

The newcomer could not believe it; he could not understand what was happening. He asked one person, "What is the matter? I cannot follow the whole sequence. They were ready to kill one another, and when the time of real action came – a man had become really angry, had lost his cool – why did the crowd disappear?"

The person said, "They are both Taoists, followers of Lao Tzu, and this is the criterion in Taoist schools: that the moment a person becomes angry he is defeated. There is no need to fight – he has shown his impotence, he has shown his fear. That's enough! His anger shows that he is a coward. Now there is no point. The other person has won the victory, he is the conqueror – he remained cool. He could not be distracted from his center. He could not be pulled out from his grounding. He remained integrated."

I know what is happening all over India – thousands of people writing against me, shouting against me – they are losing their so-called cool, which was phony, because only a phony cool can be lost. Their whole idea of tolerance, their whole idea of accepting others, of accepting different points of view is lost. A single man, who never even moves out of his room, is enough to create a turmoil in the whole country.

But it is a significant phenomenon. It shows that all those five thousand years of bogus spirituality have not done any good for India. That's what I wanted to show the whole world. They are making my point emphatically true. I am stating the point; they are supporting the argument. They are supporting me!

One man has suggested that I should be given shock treatment, electroshocks. This is real Indian culture. Another man has suggested that I should be immediately deported from the country. This is tolerance, acceptance of different points of view. The third man has suggested I should be thrown into the Arabian Sea – not even into the Indian Ocean because I might poison the Indian Ocean – into the Arabian Sea. This is a nonviolent country, the country of the seers and the sages, of the saints, mahatmas…and all kinds of dodos.

Creeping around the bedroom window, the Indian private detectives saw their client's wife in bed with another man.

"Just as I suspected," said the first Indian. "Let us go in after him."

"Great idea," the other Indian replied. "How soon do you think he will be finished?"

A traveling Indian guru, His Holiness Swami Etceterananda Paramahansa, founder of Holy Cow-Dung Ashram, Miami Beach, arrived hot, tired and thirsty at a small farm and asked the farmer, of his charity, for a drink.

"Would ye fancy a drop of ale, reverend?" asked the farmer.

The Indian guru blanched, "Nay, I would not, brother," he said sternly, "for I have taken the pledge. Not a drop of the demon drink shall pass my lips. A glass of your good, fresh milk will suffice me."

So the farmer, being a bit of a wag, fetched a glass of milk and splashed a liberal lacing of rum into it. He handed it to the guru, who drank deeply, smacked his lips, raised his eyes to heaven and said, "Oh, Lord! What a cow!"

Vacation time was suntan time as far as Joan, an admirably proportioned secretary, was concerned, and she spent almost all of her day on the roof of the Taj Mahal Hotel in Mumbai, sopping up the warm sun's rays. She wore a bathing suit the first day, but on the second she decided that no one could see her way up there, and she slipped out of it for an over-all tan.

She had hardly begun when she heard someone running up the stairs. She was lying on her stomach, so, pulling a towel over her derriere, she continued to recline as before.

"Excuse me, miss," said the flustered little assistant manager of the hotel, out of breath from running up the stairs, "the hotel does not mind your sunning on the roof, but we would very much appreciate your wearing your bathing suit as you did yesterday."

"What difference does it make?" Joan asked rather coolly. "No one can see me up here, and besides I am covered with a towel."

"I know, I know," said the embarrassed little Indian manager of the Taj Mahal hotel, "but unless you wear your bathing suit, the dinner cannot start. And the governor of Mumbai has given a big dinner to all the respectables of the city."

The woman could not understand. "What is the matter?" she said. "I don't see the point. Why can't the dinner start? What does it have to do with my bathing suit?"

"Right, lady," said the embarrassed little man. "You are lying on the dining room skylight!"

Now, how can the dinner start? All the Indians will be looking toward the heaven – they are always looking toward the heaven. Such a sight! They should not miss. But they will pretend – they may be kneeling on their knees with folded hands toward God. They will not look at the skylight directly; they will not say that they are enjoying the scene, they will do a long prayer, so long that they will forget completely about the dinner. Everybody will pretend that he is not looking at the woman lying naked on the roof.

This country is a country of pretenders, and I am hurting them. I want to hurt them, because that is the only way to pull the pus out of their centuries-old wounds. They are angry at me; they are condemning me. That shows that I am on the right track. They cannot ignore me. Either they have to be with me, or they have to be against me – either way I am willing – but I would like it to be a decisive phenomenon.

Even if a few intelligent people are with me – and they *are* with me – we can transform this whole rotten culture and give it a new life. It needs compassion. Five thousand years of spiritual, political, economic slavery... What else do you think is needed for me to be compassionate toward this culture?

They will not easily be ready to change. Change is hard; it goes against your grain; it goes against your habits; it goes against your hangover. And the hangover of India is very long. They are suffering from the past – they have only the past.

Remember one thing: a child has only the future, he has no past. Hence, a child never thinks in terms of nostalgia. There is nothing at the back. He is so fresh he has no memories. The young man lives in the present. The present is so beautiful; the past was only a childhood, a preparation at the most. And the young man does not bother about the future – one starts thinking of the future when the present starts slipping out of hand.

The old man thinks only of the past; he has no future. There is only death, a dark night waiting for him. He wants to avoid it. The only way is to turn his back toward the future and look at the past. The child looks toward the future; the old man toward the past; the young man remains in the present.

The same is true of cultures. When a culture is very new it looks to the future. It has a tremendous aspiration for the stars; it grows, it expands. When a culture becomes really young – which very rarely happens, in fact, it has not happened yet – then the culture remains in the present. And when the culture becomes old it starts thinking in terms of nostalgia, of the past, the golden age that is no more.

A youth, individually, is also a new phenomenon. In the past a child used to go from childhood to old age; youth was not at all a stage.. In the poor countries it is still so. You can see in poor countries, aboriginal tribes, children six years old, five years old, working like old men. Seven years old, eights year old, and they are already burdened with worries. They will not have a chance to be young. Hence, in the past there was no generation gap. The generation gap is a new phenomenon, a very significant phenomenon. For the first time it has happened, for the first time we have been able to afford it. It belongs to an affluent society; it belongs to a certain richness when the generation gap appears.

The child and the old man are facing each other; there is no gap. The child looks at the future; the old man looks at the past. Hence, you will always find a great friendship between children and old people. They are facing each other. That has been the case always – the children and the old people were living together. There was no gap.

The youth is a new phenomenon in the world. He is neither a child nor an old man. He is breaking new ground. He is trying to live now, here. Yes, a few individuals in the past lived in that constant youthfulness, but only individuals, not whole cultures. There is a possibility now that even a culture may start living in the present. Many individuals will be needed to prepare the ground for the culture to live in the present.

The Indian concept of time will show you many things. It says the best age has passed; it was the first age, the golden age; they call it *satyuga*, the age of truth. It was prehistoric. At that time life was the most beautiful; it was the golden peak. Time walked on four legs; it was very stable. Then the fall began.

The Indian idea of time is anti-Darwinian, unscientific, totally inhuman. Then the age began, the age of fall, not of evolution, not of progress; but things started shrinking. Time started walking on three legs. Things became hazy, unbalanced – that age is called *treta*, three legs. Then things fell even further: time had only two legs, things became even more difficult. It is called *dwapar*, two-legged time. And now is the fourth and the last stage is here, the most condemned stage: it is called *kaliyuga*. Now three legs have disappeared. Time is standing only on one leg, ready, at any moment, to fall, to be toppled. Just a one-legged man, and the one leg is already in the grave.

This is a very dark and dismal vision. This is the vision of an old, ancient, rotten country. India needs a rebirth, it needs a new childhood. It will protect its ideas because it is so accustomed to those ideas. They are its only treasure! So when I hit on those ideas I look like an enemy. The friend looks like an enemy, and the enemies are being taken as friends. But this is natural, this is logical. It can be understood.

A grave digger, thoroughly absorbed in his work, dug a pit so deep one afternoon that he could not climb out when he had finished.

Come nightfall and evening's chill, his predicament became more uncomfortable. He shouted for help and at last attracted the attention of a drunk staggering by.

"Get me out of here!" the digger pleaded. "I am cold!"

The drunk peered into the open grave and finally spotted the shivering digger in the darkness. "Well, no wonder you are cold, buddy," said the drunk, kicking some of the loose sod into the hole, "you don't have any dirt on you!"

Now, if you ask a drunkard, he will have his own logic. He will see reality in his own drunkenness.

Indians get angry because they have become accustomed to being praised continuously. Nobody has ever criticized them. Nobody has ever said to them, "You are living a death, not a life. You are shrinking and dying. You have lost the fervor, the zest, the gusto to live authentically, to live totally."

They have been praised. Their paleness has been given the halo of holiness. Their anti-life attitudes have been raised to great spiritual fantasies. Their hysterical experiences have been called *samadhi*. Their madness has been respected as if something of the beyond has descended in them. Their gibberish is thought to be esoteric; people go on finding meanings in them.

Fools have been worshipped; masochists have been thought to be ascetics; sadists have been thought to be great saints. Perversions of all kinds have been given a spiritual connotation. Now, to expose this whole lie of thousands of years is risky.

But I am willing to take the risk, because I have nothing to lose – the goose is out! I have nothing to lose. At the most they can kill me; that is not going to help them. Even my death will be of tremendous help to them. It may shock them out of their nonsense. It may bring them out of their stupor, their sleepiness.

Hence I am going to continue. They can go on criticizing me. Their criticism is basically because of my life-affirmative approach. They have lived a life-negative philosophy. They are against all that gives you joy; they are suppressive, repressive; they are boiling within, but they go on carrying a blanket cover. Nobody wants to show one's nakedness. When your blanket is so worshipped, not only in India but all over the world...

There are so many fools in the world that any Indian can find disciples. It is not a problem at all. Just being Indian is enough, and you are a guru. I have seen such things happening before my eyes.

One of my disciples, Srivastava, has now become a great spiritual leader. Now her name is long name: Her Holiness Jagatjanani – "The mother of the whole world" – Mataji Nirmalaji Srivastavaji.

She was once traveling with me in a car, and I passed by the Muktananda ashram. The people staying in Muktananda's ashram had invited me just to be there for five minutes, or so, just to take a cup of tea. It was a long journey, so I said, "There is no harm." Anyway I love a cup of tea! So I stayed for five minutes.

Nirmala saw Muktananda. She could not believe that this stupid-looking man – disgusting, more or less a buffoon – has become a great spiritual leader.

After the tea, when we entered the car, she said, "If this man can become a spiritual leader, then why cannot I become one?"

I said, "You can become one." And she has become one.

There is one man here from Australia who asked me a question, because now she is in Australia, doing great spiritual work. He asked me, "Once in a while you talk about a woman, Rabiya al-Adabiya. What do you think about Mataji Nirmala Deviji? Is she also of the same category as Rabiya al-Adabiya?" The man is here.

I know her perfectly well; for ten years she was my student. There is nothing in it, no spirituality, no meditativeness...but she got the idea from Muktananda. And it is not only one case.

You must have heard about the name of a great Sardar yogi in America, Yogi Bhajan. He was just a porter at the Delhi Airport. He saw Muktananda coming with seven hundred Americans...Of course at that time his name was Sardar Harbhajan Singh; a poor porter, but certainly he looked far better than Muktananda, more impressive.

The idea came into his mind, "If this fool can be a *paramahansa,* a *sat-guru,* etcetera, etcetera, why should I waste my time in being just a porter?" He dropped the job, went to America, and is now the greatest spiritual leader of the Sikh hierarchy in the Western hemisphere.

Just a few days ago he was back in Delhi with all his disciples. His old boss, who is a lover of mine, passed by. He saw him sitting in the lawn of the Delhi Taj Mahal Hotel with his disciples. He could not recognize him; he had changed so much. He thought, "A great mahatma."

Yogi Bhajan is a simple man in that manner, far simpler than Muktananda or Nirmala Devi. He sent a disciple to the boss and told him, "Come to my room. I have something to say to you."

The boss could not understand why the great yogi was calling him; he was thrilled, excited. He went to the room; Yogi Bhajan came in and he said, "Boss, can't you recognize me? I am just that poor Sardar Harbhajan Singh, your porter. Have you forgotten me completely?"

Then he recognized his face. He said, "But what has happened? You have become such a great yogi with so many disciples!"

Then he told the whole story, that it is due to Muktananda. The whole credit goes to Muktananda!

Indians cannot drop that garbage easily because that is the only garbage they are capable of selling to the world. They cannot get rid of that crap. It stinks! – but it sells. There are millions of people in the world who are hankering for it, and they don't know where to go. India has become their hope...and they will be exploited.

They are angry with me, all the gurus of India are angry with me, because I don't belong to their tradition. I am not here to exploit anybody; I am not here to force any indoctrination on you: Indian culture, Indian religion, and all that nonsense. I am just here to help you to be free from Christianity, Hinduism, Jainism, Buddhism. I am here to help you to be yourself, just to be yourself.

My sannyasins are not my followers, they are just my friends. I love them; they love me, but there is no hierarchy. I am not holier than you or higher than you. That goes against the Indian invest-ment. They are bound to be against me. I am affirming life, and they have been denying it all long.

Nirmala met her friend Vimala on the street one afternoon and noticed that Vimala was well along the road of pregnancy.

"You know," Nirmala said, "I would give anything to have a baby. But I guess it's hopeless."

"I know just how you feel," Vimala said. "My husband was that way too, but everything is fine now. In fact, I am eight months pregnant."

"What did you do?"

"I went to Swami Etceterananda."

"Oh, we tried that," Nirmala replied. "My husband and I went there for six months."

"Don't be silly," Vimala told her. "Go alone!"

They will find all kinds of arguments against me. They are argumentative people. For centuries they have done nothing else but make arguments. But their arguments are not going to help them, because I am not arguing for any philosophy; otherwise they would be able to refute me. I am arguing for existence, and there they are at a loss.

If it were only a philosophical argument there would be no problem.

India has known many philosophies. Buddha argued against the Vedas and there was no problem. Mahavira argued against the Upanishads; there was no problem. Shankara argued against Buddha and Mahavira; there was no problem. Ramanuja argued against Shankara; there was no problem. It is an accepted fact, if you argue only for a philosophical standpoint, nobody is worried because it is just airy-fairy; it does not make any change in life.

I am arguing not for a philosophy. I am not philosophical at all, I am totally existential. That's where they are finding it difficult. They are finding it absolutely difficult to cope with me – what to do with me. Hence the anger, hence the condemnation, hence all kinds of third-rate criticism. They simply show their reality. Those third-rate criticisms that they go on making against me are simply bringing their reality to the surface. They are showing their nakedness, their ugliness. And that's serving my purpose.

The real estate salesmen in Mumbai lead lives entirely unbounded by mere prosaic fact. One of these gentlemen was showing some property to a possible rich customer, and he was pulling out all the stops.

He finished up with, "Why, the climate is the best in the country! Do you know? – no one ever dies here."

And just then a funeral procession came into view, wound slowly down the street and disappeared from sight. The real estate agent was taken aback for a second, but he made a quick recovery.

Removing his hat, he said solemnly, "Poor old undertaker – starved to death."

Indians are clever in argumentation. If I were arguing they would have found a thousand and one arguments. But I am not arguing, I am simply pointing to the moon. My fingers are not my arguments but only indicators. Don't cling to my fingers, see the moon. It is time that the moon should be seen.

You ask me, "Even so, you keep hammering this rotten culture..." I will go on hammering. It is so rotten that there is every hope that we may get rid of it. It is falling apart on its own; just a little hammering is needed. I am going to hit it mercilessly.

You ask: "What is this business?" This is the business of people like me. It has always been the business of people like me.

Socrates was told by the court in Athens, "If you stop talking about truth, we can release you. You will not be put to death."

Socrates refused, and the words he used were very beautiful. He said, "That is my business. I cannot stop talking about truth. Just as I breathe, I talk about truth. It is my business."

I am going to continue. My hammering will become harder because I have to bring more and more rubbish to the surface. My hammering will go deeper. It is a surgical hammering: many rotten parts of this god-damned country have to be removed. It needs nothing less than that. Medicines won't help; it needs operation. And I am preparing the operating table...

It is going to be a great adventure. Even if the patient dies, there is no harm. At least there must be some space, at least there must be a little less of a crowd. Anyway, the patient is dead This country is living a posthumous existence. It has died long ago: the day it started the idea that we are falling down, that the golden age is lost, that we are falling deeper and deeper into darkness and hell – it lost all qualities of life. Since then it is a posthumous existence.

My effort is to give this country a real death so that a real birth becomes possible. Resurrection is possible only after crucifixion.

There is no other way. Death is the way of life coming back, so don't be afraid of death! In fact, life and death are not opposites, they are not contradictions to each other. They are like two wings: they help each other, they are complementary.

I teach you to live totally, and I also teach you to die totally. Totality has to be the taste of a really religious person. When I say "really religious person" I don't mean anything supernatural, anything higher, holier. I simply mean the innocent life, the ordinary life. I exalt the ordinary, I praise the ordinary, I worship the ordinary.

Enough for today.

only one time: now

The first question:

Osho,
I have heard you say not to ask for anything in our prayers. Then why does Jesus say to us, "When you pray, say: Give us our daily bread. Forgive us our trespasses. Lead us not into temptation, but deliver us from evil"? And also Jesus himself asked, "My father, if it is possible, let this cup pass me by, yet not as I will, but as thou wilt."
Please explain.

Religion has a long history. Much of it is only a hangover from the past. The real religion, the essential religion is only possible now, because man has come of age. Past humanity was very childish – not child-like, remember, but childish. It was bound to be so; it was inevitable, unavoidable. So I am not complaining about it I am simply stating the fact that whenever you think of religion, never think in terms of the past; otherwise you will have a totally wrong orientation. Think more in terms of the present.

When you think of the Theory of Relativity, you don't bring

Newton in. You know he did contribute something to scientific growth, but his days are over. We are grateful for whatsoever he did, whatsoever he could, but with Albert Einstein, Newton is finished. He will remain only a footnote in the history of scientific growth.

The same is true about religion, about every human endeavor. When you are going to the moon in a spaceship, certainly the man who invented the bullock cart has contributed immensely. Without the bullock cart there would have not been any possibility for the spaceship, but you don't go on worshiping the man who invented the bullock cart. You don't even remember his name. While you are involved with a spaceship, it is better to forget all about the bullock cart. They are not going to help; their mechanism is out of date.

But about religion we are not so rational; about religion we are very emotional. About religion we are not so scientific. About religion we are very illogical, superstitious.

Religion has passed through two phases. The first phase was of prayer; that is the bullock cart era of religion. The second phase is meditation, that is the spaceship age of religion. They are totally different dimensions. Their sources are different, their workings are different, their whole milieu is different. And one should not get confused between the two.

There is much confusion around the world, so let me explain to you. Be very patient because we are all conditioned by the religions of prayer. Their weight is heavy; every human being is crushed under a mountainous weight. The work for a master has become more and more difficult, because it is not only a question of helping you to be meditative: before that can start much has to be negated in you, much rubbish has to be shoveled, much dirt has to be cleaned out. The whole past has to be dismantled; only then will you be able to open your wings to the essential, mature, adult dimension of religion.

Prayer means fear, hence all the old religions are fear-oriented. Their God is nothing but a creation of their fear; it is not a discovery, it is imagination, it is projection. They are full of fear; they need a father figure to protect them from all kinds of fear. There are thousands of fears in life: there are anxieties, anguishes, problems to be encountered, unsolvable puzzles, unbridgeable gaps, and man is surrounded by great darkness. He needs a protective hand. He wants somebody as a security, as a safety.

Each child is brought up by his parents. His first experience with his parents becomes very decisive, because he is protected, comforted, consoled. All his needs are fulfilled; he has no worries, he has no responsibilities, he is taken care of. He can rely on his parents. But he is not going to have this forever, so sooner or later he will have to stand on his own feet.

The moment he stands on his own feet a great trembling arises in him: now who is going to save him? Now who is going to console him? The problems go on becoming bigger and bigger every day. As life progresses it starts coming closer to death, which is the ultimate problem to be solved. And there is great anxiety about death.

Each child starts falling back; each child starts going back to the childhood state because that seems to be the only part of his life where there was not a single problem at all. This is regression.

This regression has been thought as prayer; it is not prayer. Then he falls on his knees and starts praying to a god...

It is not accidental that all the religions call God "the Father." Yes, there are a few other religions which call God "the Mother" – which is the same. In matriarchal societies God is the Mother; in patriarchal societies God is the Father. One thing is certain: that God has to be the ultimate parent.

Every community, society, civilization, invents its own God; they say, "God created man in his own image." That is absolutely wrong – man has created God in *his* own image. And because there are so many kinds of people in the world, there are so many kinds of images of God.

That image is your fabrication, and you are praying before your own invention. Prayer is really one of the most absurd things possible. It is as if you are praying before a mirror, seeing your own face, kneeling down before your own image, asking for favors, and there is nobody in the mirror except your reflection. All prayer...prayer as such is juvenile, it is regressive.

This will hurt you but I cannot help it: I have to say the truth as it is.

You ask me: "I heard you say not to ask for anything in our prayers." In fact, the moment you stop asking, you will stop praying. That is a simple methodology – I have to go sometimes a little roundabout not to hurt you too much.

I don't see that there is any God who created the world. I certainly experience a quality of godliness in existence, but it is a quality, not a person. It is more like love, more like silence, more like joy – less like a person. You are never going to meet God and say hello to him – how are you going to? I have been looking for you for thousands of years; where have you been hiding?

God is not a person but only a presence. When I say "presence" be very attentive, because you can go on listening according to your own conditioning. You can even make presence something objective – you have again fallen into the same trap. God is a presence at the innermost core of your being: it is your *own* presence. It is not a meeting with somebody else.

Martin Buber, one of the great Jewish thinkers of this age, has written that prayer is a dialogue between "I" and "thou." There is no "thou"; hence the dialogue is impossible. All prayers are monologues. Because there is no "thou" there is no "I" either; they can exist only together, they cannot exist in separation. How can you imagine the existence of "I" without "thou"? "Thou's" are needed to delineate the line of the "I."

Martin Buber in a sense is right – he is defining the whole past of religion. He himself is burdened with the past; he could never get out of his Jewish skin. He remained encaged, he remained a Jew – a nice, beautiful person, of great intellectual capacities, but still in bondage.

The Jewish idea of "I" and "thou" is a basic pattern for prayer. Without "I" you cannot pray because there is nobody to pray. Without "thou" you cannot pray, because to whom do you pray? If you are not asking for anything, then what you are praying for? Prayer means asking: it is a demand, however camouflaged, however subtly hidden behind beautiful garbs and masks. But it is an asking; you are demanding, you are saying, "Give me this! Give me that!"

So when I say there is no God, remember it: I really mean that existence is enough unto itself. It needs no creator. There is creativity but no creator. The division between a creator and creativity has to be dissolved; only then you will be able to rise to the peaks of meditation. Otherwise, you will remain confined to the childish patterns of the past: kneeling down before images in temples, in synagogues, in churches, and doing all kinds of foolish things. Since those foolish things are being done by thousands of others, you never become aware that they are foolish. When the crowd is with you, when the multitudes are with you, you feel on safe ground. You feel shaky only when you are alone.

Meditation is the experience of aloneness. Only very courageous people can enter into that dimension. Prayer is a crowd phenomenon, it is part of the collective mind. When you are in a crowd, certainly a great confidence arises in you. It is infectious, because so many people cannot be wrong.

I would like to tell you: it is always the case that the multitudes are bound to be wrong. Only rarely an individual is right, because truth is such a pinnacle, such a peak, like Everest. You cannot go to Everest with a multitude; there is not space enough. Only one person can stand on the highest peak, alone.

Meditation is the experience of being totally alone, utterly alone. Prayer is a crowd phenomenon; it is mob psychology. Hence Hinduism, Christianity, Judaism, Mohammedanism, all have remained religions of prayer. Two religions which tried to become religions of meditation fell back. Buddhism and Jainism, two religions tried to be religions of meditation – but only Buddha and Mahavira, two individuals, could manage it. The moment they died their religions started falling back to the old, regressive pattern; they all became religions of prayer.

Now Jainas are praying before Mahavira. That is even worse, because Christians can have some support from Jesus; Jainas have no support from Mahavira. Buddhists, millions of Buddhists, are praying before the statue of Buddha. That is ridiculous, unbelievable, because Buddha's last words were, "Be a light unto yourself." And it is a strange phenomenon that the Buddha's statues were the first to be made in the world; his statues were the first to be installed in temples.

There are temples of Buddha with thousands of statues. One temple in China is called Ten Thousand Buddhas Temple – ten thousand statues of Buddha in one temple! The whole mountain has been carved into a temple. If Buddha comes back he will start beating his head, he will commit suicide.

The first thing to be remembered: I believe in an organismic universe. There are no divisions as the creator and the created, as the higher and the lower, as the sacred and the profane, as this and that. I believe in one organism.

Existence cannot be thought of in terms of a painter and his painting, because the moment the painting is finished, the painter and painting become two separate entities. Existence has to be thought of only in terms of a dancer and his dance. You cannot separate them; the dancer and the dance are one. At the highest peak of dancing, the dancer disappears into the dance – there is no dancer but only dance.

That is the experience of meditation: when you dissolve yourself into existence, when the dewdrop slips into the ocean and becomes the ocean. And vice versa is also true: the ocean slips into the dewdrop and becomes the dewdrop. They cannot be conceived as two entities any more.

So when I say God is not a presence, I mean he's not anything outside you – neither a person nor a presence, as thought of in the language of objectivity. When I say God is a presence, I simply mean he is the innermost core of your being – that silent core, that space where nobody else can enter into you; that private, that absolute, intimate, virgin space, your interiority, is godliness.

The word *God* can create trouble for you. Words are very troublesome because words carry the past; they are made by the past, they are overburdened by the past. Any word is dangerous, because its meaning comes from the past. And for me the problem is: to use the words which come from the past – because there are no other words – but to give them such a twist and turn that they can give you a little insight into a new meaning. The words are old, the bottles are old, but the wine is new.

An old lady who was walking her dog decided to go into the local supermarket, which did not allow dogs. She tied the animal to a fire hydrant. No sooner was the dog tied than every dog in the neighborhood that was loose, started sniffing this defenseless animal. The cop on the corner, observing what was happening, called to the old woman and told her that she could not leave her dog there alone.

She asked him why and he replied, "Lady, your dog is in heat."

She answered, "Eat? She'll eat anything."

He countered, "The dog should be bred."

The old lady replied, "She'll eat bread, cake – anything you give her she will eat."

In complete frustration he said, "That dog should be laid!"

The old woman stared directly into his eyes and answered, "So lay her! I always wanted a police dog."

Words are dangerous...every possibility of being misunderstood.

You say: "I heard you say not to ask for anything in our prayers." In fact, that is my way to prevent you from praying. If you have nothing to ask for, why should you pray? Then what is the rationale of it?

Even a man like Jesus is in many ways childish. It cannot be helped: he belonged to the bullock cart age of religion; he belonged to the Judaic tradition. He lived as a Jew, he talked as a Jew, he died as a Jew. His whole way of thinking, looking, observing, was purely Jewish.

He is not really in rebellion, he is not a rebel in the true sense of the word. On the contrary, he was trying to prove that he belongs to the tradition; he was trying to prove that he is the person who has been predicted by the old prophets, that he has come to fulfill all their prophecies. Now this is sheer nonsense! Nobody can predict for anybody else; the past is absolutely impotent to know anything of the future. The future is that which remains open. If it can be predicted it becomes closed, it is no more the future; if you can predict the future it is already past. You have already canceled its opening, it has become closed.

He was trying to convince the Jews: "I am the messiah you have been waiting for." He was trying in every way to fulfill their expectations: doing all kinds of miracles, trying in every possible way to argue for his case. This is not the way of a revolutionary. The revolutionary simply disconnects himself from the past; he has nothing to do with the past.

He was still trying to be a prophet in the Jewish sense. A prophet is a religious man with political tendencies. Religion and politics are un-mixable. If you mix them you will create a hodgepodge. That's what Jesus did: on the one hand he was trying to be religious; on the other hand he was trying to prove that he is a prophet like the old prophets. This political tendency and the religious leaning became a very confused phenomenon. He was utterly confused.

I don't see much clarity in him; he's not transparent, he's very clouded. You can see it in his own statement. He says, "My Father, if it is possible, let this cup pass me by…" That is his innermost desire. Otherwise, why should he say, "My Father, if it is possible, let this cup pass me by, yet not as I will, but as thou wilt"? This is a contradiction, a clear-cut contradiction. This is not said by a truly surrendered person. A truly surrendered person has nothing to say – whatsoever is happening is happening.

Whence comes this "if" – "*if* it is possible"? This desire is there that "if you can manage, please…but if you cannot manage then it is okay; then whatsoever happens I will accept." But there is reluctance, there is contradiction. His own desire is that this cup should pass by – this agony, this crucifixion, this death, should pass by. He was really deep down waiting for a miracle; he was hoping for a miracle. He was not very different from the crowd that had gathered there to observe the crucifixion. He was not very different from the rabbis and the priests and the government who were all conspiring to kill him; their philosophical background was the same.

The rabbis and the high priests of the temple of Jerusalem were trying to prove "this man is a fake." And he was trying to prove that "No, I am the true messiah – and at the last moment you will see, when God himself will descend to save his only begotten son." Time started passing: he is nailed, he is crucified, he is waiting for the miracle. Nothing is happening, all expectations are turning sour. In that moment of agony he screams, "Why have you forsaken me?"

There is nobody to whom he is calling. There is nobody who has forsaken him. It was his own idea; it was his own projection, it was his own hallucination. This state is hysterical! He was waiting to the last moment. And when he said, "If it is not possible, then let thy will be done," that is surrender, but not true: with reluctance, just a face-saving device.

Nothing is happening, all is finished. The crowd is jeering and laughing at the whole scene, people are throwing stones, insulting him, hurting him. People are returning home very frustrated because nothing has happened, convinced that he was a fake. Even his own disciples escaped, seeing that, now it was dangerous to be there. If they were caught...if Jesus was not saved by God, who was going to save them? Poor fellows – they escaped. And it is logical.

Jesus saying, "Let thy will be done," is just making a last effort to save his face. This is not the way of a surrendered man. How can you surrender to your own projection?

Hence, I don't teach you prayer; prayer is bound to be diametrically opposite to what I teach. Its expectation is basically contradictory: it requires you to surrender, only can it then be fulfilled. And when you surrender, then what is there left to be fulfilled? If there is some demand still to be fulfilled, you are not surrendered. Please see the contradiction.

Prayer is asking of you something impossible. You can ask God anything, but first you surrender totally. If you are surrendered totally then there is no point in asking. Whence comes the asking? Who will demand? And if you are still demanding, the surrender is missing, so prayer cannot be fulfilled.

You see the simple mechanism of it? A prayer can be fulfilled only if you don't ask anything. But then what is there to be fulfilled? You had not asked in the first place.

I teach you a totally different kind of religiousness. It is of meditation. You are not to worship, you are not to pray; you have to go deep within your own self – a journey of self-discovery. It is not a question of discovering God. Why you are after God? What wrong has he done to you? Forgive him; forget him!

The first and the only inquiry worth anything is to know: "Who am I within this body-mind mechanism? What is this consciousness, this miracle of consciousness?" This miracle of awareness has to be discovered. You have to peel your being as one peels an onion. Go on peeling...you will find layers within layers. And finally, when all layers are discarded, eliminated, you will find in your hands pure nothingness, emptiness, *shunyata*. That is your essential core, the center of the cyclone.

Discarding the layers of the onion you have discarded the bottle that was created by you, by the society, by the culture, by the past, by tradition, and when you have discarded the bottle, the goose is out. Then you are as infinite as the universe itself, as eternal as timelessness itself.

You can call it godliness – it *is* godliness. It is the highest, the greatest flowering of being. But it is not a God somewhere outside you. You cannot pray to it. You can *be* it, but you cannot pray *to* it, because it is not separate.

You ask me: "Then why does Jesus say to us, 'When you pray, say...'?" Jesus has never said this to *you*. He was talking to other kinds of people. If Jesus comes to you, remember one thing: there will be no possibility of any communication between you and him. There will be a gap of two thousand years. And you know very well even the small gap between you and your father is almost unbridgeable. Talk to your father and you are talking to a wall. Your father feels the same: talking to a child is impossible; there seems to be no communication.

Two thousand years is a big gap. If Jesus comes right now he will look like a pygmy to you. You will not be able to understand why this man has been worshipped for two thousand years...for what? You will not be able at all to appreciate him. You will find a thousand and one faults in him, very easily. Even the most stupid of you will be able to see that: "Is this the man we have been worshiping in thousands of churches, millions of people praying to him? Is this the man?"

Two thousand years of continuous painting…and that is the work of the church, theologians, philosophers, priests – they go on making it up to date, as far as they can, they go on putting new layers of paint. If you dig deep into these thick layers of paint you will be really at a loss. When you discover Jesus you will be very frustrated. You will find a very ordinary man. Yes, in those days he was extraordinary – it is a question of time. In those days he was extraordinary because the people were even far more backward than he was.

But now you are two thousand years ahead of him. The way he speaks and the things he says he is not saying to you.

You say "he says to us." No, he has no idea of you. What I am saying I am saying to you, but what Jesus said he was saying to the people of his time. He is not contemporary to you, how can he say anything to *you*?

This is one of the problems that I encounter every day, because the people who come to me are living with the hangover of Jesus or of Buddha or of Mahavira or of Krishna or of Zarathustra. They have their past hangovers, and I am a contemporary man! I am simply talking to the twentieth century, and not only to the twentieth century crowd, but to the twentieth century elite – the people of the highest intelligence. Hence, it is difficult to understand what I am saying.

You live thousands of years in the past. It is very rare to find a contemporary man. Somebody is one thousand years old, somebody two thousand, somebody three thousand… And the older they are, they think the more valuable they are. Hindus try to prove that their Vedas are the oldest scriptures, as if this is something creditable. The oldest scripture simply means that you have not moved since then, that you're still carrying the burden. Historians say that the scriptures of the Hindus, the Vedas, are five thousand years old. Hindus are not ready to accept that – they say they are at least ninety thousand years old. The older they are the better.

The same is true about other religions, as if all that is old is gold. In fact, life is always new, fresh, as fresh as dewdrops in the early morning sun on the lotus leaf, as fresh as the stars, as fresh as the eyes of a newly-born baby, as fresh as the song birds right now.

Life knows only one time, that is now.

Jesus was not talking to you, he could not – he had no idea about you; he could not conceive of you. But he was talking to his own people, and his people lived with these ideas. He was paraphrasing the Jewish concept of religion. He was saying: "Give us our daily bread. Forgive us our trespasses. Lead us not into temptation, but deliver us from evil."

Now, to me all that is just sheer rubbish – "Give us our daily bread."

In the past, humanity has been very poor. The whole past has been of long starvation, hunger, illness, famine, floods – all kinds of diseases. It is a miracle how man has survived somehow.

In countries like India, that is still the case. Hence, you will see one thing happening: the intelligent core of Western youth is turning more and more toward meditation, but the Eastern masses are turning more and more toward Christianity. Indians would like more Mother Teresas in India than me. Naturally, because bread is needed. If you look around India you will find only the poor people being converted to Christianity; not a single rich man is converted to Christianity. Beggars, orphans, widows, aboriginals, who cannot manage even one meal every day, they are being converted to Christianity. It appeals to them because bread is their problem.

Jesus says, "Give us our daily bread." We have to create it; there is nobody to give it. That is the work of science; religion has nothing to do with it. We should start marking lines: what can be done by science should be done by science; what can be done by technology should be done by technology. If your car has stopped and you have run out of gas, you don't just kneel down by the car and start praying, "Give us our daily gas." That will be as stupid as this prayer. You know you have to search for a gas pump! This is not the way – it is not going to happen.

But priests have been trying all along to make religion dominate your whole life – from bread to God. They are very much afraid of dividing; hence, they were against science, against technology.

Bertrand Russell is right when he says that "If the whole of humanity is well fed, well nourished, prayers like this – 'Give us our daily bread' – will become absolutely futile." There will be no need at all! And with that your churches, your temples, your priests, will start losing their power. They have possessed humanity for the simple

reason that they have not allowed science and technology to improve
your lot.

In India, Mahatma Gandhi was against science, against very
necessary science too. He was against the railway train, telegraph,
post office, electricity. He wanted this country to live at least as
primitively as ten thousand years ago people used to live. The only
thing that he accepted as the greatest scientific invention was the
spinning wheel. And he was worshipped as a mahatma.

To me, he is doing a crime, a far bigger crime than Adolf Hitler.
But his crime is very subtle. You cannot detect it because he is
talking in religious garbage: "One should trust God – why should one
trust science?"

My emphasis is this: life is a multidimensional phenomenon, and
we should be very clear cut about divisions. Music should be taken
care of by musicians, not by mathematicians. Dancing should be
taken care of by dancers, not by chemists. Poetry should be taken
care of by poets, not by physiologists. Science has its own contribution – it is man's intelligence. There is no need for any prayer; we can
provide this earth with a paradise, but we will not be able unless we
stop all kinds of nonsense that we are stuffed with.

This has been a strategy of the priest. He can dominate you only if
you are poor; he can dominate you only if you are starving – because
when you are poor and starving and miserable, you are bound to fall
at his feet because he is the mediator between God and you. You don't
know the address where God lives, what language he speaks. That is
the expertise of the priest. He knows God speaks Sanskrit, and he
does not allow you to learn Sanskrit either, because if *you* learn
Sanskrit then he will not be needed. He knows God speaks Aramaic,
Hebrew; he will not allow you to learn Aramaic and Hebrew. If you
learn them then he will be exposed, because there is nothing in
Aramaic or Hebrew or Sanskrit, nothing of any value.

If you don't know those languages you remain ignorant, and he
goes on pretending to be the wise man. He can go on leading you –
blind people are leading other blind people. His power depends on
you, and he has become very cunning. Centuries of exploitation
have given him the craft, the art, the knack of exploiting you.

Sigmund Steinberg, the well-known importer of ladies' gloves,
paid an unexpected call on the rabbi of his temple. That worthy

was more than pleased to see his fabulously wealthy congregate, who more than made up in contributions what he lacked in attendance and religious zeal. This time, however, the trip to temple was for a completely religious, if rather unusual, reason.

"Rabbi," Steinberg commenced after the usual amenities, "I am here to see you about someone most near and dear to me. My own, my darling, my three-times-a-champion, Westminster Abbey the Third, mine little poodle is this coming Tisha B'Av thirteen years old, and I want, Rabbi, you should bar mitzvah him."

The rabbi was completely taken aback. "But my dear Mr. Steinberg, that is impossible. There has never been in the history of the Jewish religion such a thing. It would be a scandal. The temple would be a laughingstock. My orders would be revoked. The sisterhood would be disbanded. The building campaign would be halted. The gentiles would be hysterical. And the board of directors would have my neck."

Steinberg was unmoved. Without so much as the bat of an eyelash, he addressed the rabbi again. "For the occasion, I am donating to the temple the amount, in cash, of five thousand dollars."

"Mr. Steinberg," the rabbi beamed, "why didn't you tell me in the first place that the dog is Jewish?"

These people have become really cunning. Their whole effort is how to remain in power, and the most necessary thing to remain in power, to remain rich, to remain in domination, is to keep humanity suffering. That is a simple strategy; anybody who has eyes can see it. Just think of a world where people are blissful, ecstatic, where people are living moment-to-moment with a dance and with a song... How many of your old religions will remain? How many of your temples and churches and synagogues will be able to survive? They will start disappearing like smoke.

As your suffering disappears, your so-called religions will disappear. They *are* opium for the people; they have been keeping you in a subtle unconscious state. They are giving you great hopes. Those hopes are nothing but drugs, far more dangerous than any chemical drug can be. They have drugged the whole of humanity.

Jesus says, "Give us our daily bread. Forgive us our trespasses." What trespasses? The whole of religion has lived with the idea of sin.

What was the sin of Adam and Eve? – they disobeyed.

Disobedience is not a sin; disobedience is part of growth. Each child has to disobey his parents, sooner or later – and the sooner the better, because life is short. You should not waste your time. One has to learn to say *no* definitively; only then can a point arise where one can say *yes*. Without being able to say *no*, nobody is capable of saying *yes*. Disobedience is the background in which real obedience blossoms.

If anybody was responsible for original sin it was God, not the poor serpent – he is the greatest benefactor of humanity, the first true messiah, because he seduced Adam and Eve and told them to disobey. He was the first master. Without him there would have been no humanity, no Jesus, no Buddha, no Confucius, no Lao Tzu. The whole credit goes to the poor serpent. And the whole cause of sin is God himself: he prohibited…

The Garden of Eden is a big garden. There were only two trees which he was afraid that Adam and Eve might start eating from their fruits. One was the tree of knowledge and the other was the tree of life. Now, why should God be afraid of knowing and living?

You can see the whole strategy of the priest. He is afraid of two things: knowing and living. He prevents you from knowing so that he remains the knower, and he prevents you from living so that you are always falling at his feet, begging: "Give us our daily bread." He does not allow you to live totally, intensely. He hinders you in every possible way; he cripples you; he paralyzes you. And the whole story begins in the Garden of Eden.

God seems to be the first priest. Why should he be afraid of knowing? He really should have blessed them; he should have told Adam and Eve, "The first thing you have to do is go to these two trees; they are the most valuable. Know – know life in its totality, know its mysteries, explore. Go from the known to the unknown, from the unknown to the unknowable – go on a long pilgrimage. Nothing should be left unknown. You should become part of the whole mystery of the universe." That should have been his first advice if he was really loving and compassionate.

He should have told them, "Live – and live passionately, and live totally! Live intensely; live ecstatically! These are the two trees you should not miss."

If I had been in his place, this would have been my advice to you: "Live under these trees. You can enjoy other trees whenever you want – just for a change you can go anywhere, but these two trees should not be forgotten." Instead of saying this, God says, "Don't eat from the tree of knowledge." Why? Is he afraid that if Adam and Eve become knowers then they will become equal to him? Is he afraid of Adam and Eve becoming buddhas, awakened?

Knowing comes through meditation, remember. The tree of knowing is the tree of meditation, and God prohibits meditation. Knowing comes as you enter deeper into your being; when you have reached to the very core, knowing explodes. You become flooded with infinite light.

The same is true about living: the more you know, the more you live; the more you live, the more you know. They go together, hand in hand, dancing. Knowing and living are two aspects of the same coin; both happen to the meditator. But a religion which is based on fear is afraid of both.

This is my whole teaching here: know and live. Live without fear; know without hesitation.

The serpent seems to be absolutely right because he says to Adam and Eve, "God is afraid. If you eat from this tree of knowledge you will become like gods – then there will be no superiority, you will be equal to God. If you eat from the tree of life you will become immortals, just as gods are immortals. And God is afraid. He wants to keep you in subjugation."

Now who has committed the sin? Who has trespassed – God, or Adam and Eve? But Jesus still thinks in terms of a rotten past. He is still thinking that man has trespassed.

I don't see…whatsoever you are doing is natural. What trespasses are you doing? The instincts that you are living are given by nature. Your sex is a gift from nature, your joy for nourishing food is part of your nature. You would like to live beautifully, you would love to live comfortably. You would like to have a beautiful garden around your house, you would like a warm swimming pool. You would like to love a man or a woman. I don't see that there is any trespassing. You are not committing any sin, you are simply following your nature, your spontaneous tendencies.

Religions have condemned you, utterly condemned you. They have condemned everything that is natural, and through that condemnation they have created great guilt in you. Your whole heart is full of guilt. That guilt pulls you back; it does not allow you to live totally in anything. It does not allow your dance to reach to its peak, to its crescendo. It does not allow you to sing and shout and rejoice. It represses you.

I cannot support any such ideas.

Jesus says, "Lead us not into temptation." What temptation is he talking about? What temptations are there? Life is so simple! But you can label things as temptations, then they become temptations.

For example, I was born in a Jaina family, unfortunately, but nothing can be done about it. One has to choose one unfortunate state or another. Up to my eighteenth year I had not tasted a poor tomato, because Jainas are absolutely vegetarian, and the poor tomato has the color of meat – just the color! There is nothing in it, but the very color is enough for Jainas to feel repulsion. Tomatoes were not brought into my house; I had not tasted them.

When I was eighteen years old I went for a picnic with a few of my Hindu friends. I was the only Jaina, and they were all Hindus. I had not eaten in the night up to that time either, because Jainas don't eat in the night – that is a great sin, because in the night a mosquito may fall into your food, some insect may crawl in, and unknowingly you may have eaten something alive. That will drag you to hell. So one has to eat in the day when the light is absolutely clear. One may not even drink in the night, even water, because in the night – who knows? – something without any conscious effort on your part may be killed.

So I had not eaten in the night, and I had not tasted tomatoes up to my eighteenth year. They were great temptations. I had seen tomatoes in the market, and they were really tempting – sitting so meditatively, so centered, so grounded. Potatoes are also not allowed in Jaina families because they grow underneath the ground, and anything that grows in darkness is dangerous to eat because it will bring darkness to your soul.

When I went for this picnic to a hill station, all my friends were enjoying the mountains and the beauty and the castles, and nobody was in a hurry to prepare food. I am a lazy man – from the very beginning – I cannot cook food. I can cook many other things…but I cannot cook food, not even my tea. So I had to wait until they decided to eat.

I was feeling hungry – the journey, the traveling, and the mountains' fresh air. I was feeling hungry, and the night was coming closer, and I was feeling afraid also: "What is going to happen? If they cook food in the night, then I have to sleep without food." And my stomach was hurting.

Then they started cooking food. Great temptations: tomatoes, potatoes, and the beautiful smell of the food. I was wavering between temptation and virtue. One moment I thought, "It is better to sleep one night without food – one cannot die – rather than suffer in hell and hellfire just for a few tomatoes and a few potatoes."

But then the hunger was too much. Then the argument came to me: "If all my friends are going to hell, what am I going to do in heaven? It is better to be with my friends in hell than to be with those foolish Jaina saints in heaven. At least in hell you can cook tomatoes, potatoes, you can eat well, there is enough fire. Even I can cook."

They all tried to persuade me: "There is nobody else here, and we are not going to tell your family either. Nobody will ever come to know that you have eaten in the night, and that you have eaten tomatoes or potatoes."

Reluctantly, hesitatingly, I agreed. I could not sleep until I had vomited in the middle of the night. Nobody else vomited – they were all fast asleep and snoring – only I vomited. It was my psychology, because I was suffering from the idea that I had committed a sin. It was not the tomatoes that I vomited, it was my attitude. And that day it became clear, absolutely clear, that you can only live life totally if you drop all attitudes. Otherwise you will live partially, and to live partially is not to live at all.

I cannot support this prayer.

Jesus says, "Lead us not into temptation." One thing is certain: that Jesus is feeling temptation, otherwise why this prayer? He is feeling that God is leading him into temptation. If God is leading, why not surrender? Then the real prayer should have been: "Lead us really into total temptation. When you are leading, why do it half-heartedly? When you have decided to lead, then lead us totally!"

He is tempted; his prayer is an absolute confirmation of his temptation. It is natural – he was a human being just like you, as alive as you are. And he must have felt all natural likings, dislikings. He must have loved things, he must have preferred things. But he was afraid – the past was heavy on him.

"Lead us not into temptation, but deliver us from evil." There is no evil, hence there is no need to be delivered from anything. There is only one thing, and that is a state of unconsciousness, unknowing, unawareness. I will not call it evil – it is a situation, a challenge, an adventure. It is not evil. Existence is not evil, existence is an opportunity to grow. And, of course, the opportunity to grow is possible only if you are tempted into thousands of ways, if you are called forth by unknown aspirations, if a tremendous desire in you arises to explore... And the only thing that can prevent you is unconsciousness, unawareness. That too is a great challenge – to conquer it.

Become more conscious, become more aware, become more alive. Let all your juices flow. Don't hold yourself back. Respect your nature, love yourself and don't be worried about unnecessary things. Unworried, move into the thickness of life, explore it. Yes, you will commit many mistakes – so what? One learns through committing mistakes. Yes, you will make many errors – so what? It is only by going into errors that one comes to the right door. Before one knocks at the right door, one has to knock on thousands of wrong doors. That is part of the game, part of the play.

Mr. and Mrs. Goldberg had scrimped and saved to put their eldest son through college. At last, they had the money and decided to send him to a fine highbrow Eastern boarding school. They saw him off on the train, and tearfully bade him farewell.

A few months later he returned home for the Christmas holidays. The parents were overjoyed to have their son Sammy back with them. The mother greeted him with, "Samelah, oh, it's so good to see you."

"Mother," he replied, "stop calling me Samelah. After all, I'm a grown man now, and I do wish you would refer to me as Samuel."

She apologized and asked, "I hope you only ate kosher foods while you were away?"

"Mother, we are living in the modern age, and it's preposterous to hang on to old-world traditions. I indulged in all types of food, kosher and non-kosher, and believe me, you would be better off if you did."

"Well, tell me, did you at least go to the synagogue to offer a prayer of thanks occasionally?"

The son replied, "Really, do you honestly feel going to a synagogue, when you are associating with a large percentage of non-Jews, is the proper thing to do? Honestly, Mother, it is unfair to ask it of me, really."

At this point, Mrs. Goldberg, fighting back anger, looked at her eldest son and said, "Tell me, Samuel, are you still circumcised?"

The past goes on hanging around you. It is an imprisonment.

If you are a Jew or a Christian or a Hindu or a Jaina or a Buddhist, you are not really a man. You are dead, you are a corpse – circumcised or not circumcised.

One becomes alive only when one is totally free from the past. To be in the present is the only way to be alive.

These prayers are nothing but fear-oriented people's projections and desires. I teach you love, not fear.

In all the languages of the world, the religious person is called God-fearing. That is an ugly expression; it should be dropped. For the religious person it is impossible to be God-fearing, because he cannot have fear. A religious person simply lives lovingly, not out of fear. These are all prayers out of fear: "Give us our daily bread. Forgive us our trespasses. Lead us not into temptation, but deliver us from evil."

Drop all this. Be a little more alive, a little more contemporary.

Henry went on his first hunting trip. When he got back to his office, his partner Morris could not wait to hear all about the trip. Henry told him, "Well, I went into the woods with the guide. You know me, two minutes in the woods, I get lost. I am walking extra quiet, when all of a sudden the biggest bear you ever did see is standing right in front of me. I turn around and run just as fast as I can and that bear, he is running even faster.

"Just when I feel his hot breath on my neck, he slipped and fell. I jumped over a brook and kept running, but I was losing my breath and sure enough there was that bear getting close to me again. He was almost on top of me when he slipped again and fell. I kept on running and finally I found myself in the clearing of the woods. The bear was running as fast as he could and I knew I did not stand a chance. I saw the other hunters and shouted for help and just then the bear slipped and fell again. My guide was able to take aim and he shot the bear and killed him."

Morris said, "Henry, that was quite a story. You are a very brave man. If that would have happened to me, I would have made in my pants."

Henry looked at him and shrugged, "Morris, what do you think the bear was slipping on?"

Man has lived in fear; it is time to put a full stop to it. Humanity needs a new dawn, a totally new vision.

Jesus says God is love. I would like to change that. I would like to say, "Love is God." When you say God is love, love is only one of the qualities of God; he may have other qualities: wisdom, justice, etcetera. To me, love is God; godliness is only one of the qualities of love. There is no other God than the fragrance of love. But the fragrance can arise only in deep meditation, not in prayer. Prayer stinks of fear.

I know perfectly well that to say anything against Jesus or Buddha or Krishna hurts you, but I cannot help it. If it hurts, it hurts. Rather than feeling sour about what I say, ponder over it, meditate over it. Because I am not interested in arguing with anybody. I have tremendous love for Jesus, Buddha, Mahavira, Krishna. They were beautiful people, but their days are finished.

We need new insights, new pastures, new dimensions. These new dimensions are bound to go against our old, rotten mind. So when it hurts, remember: it is not the truth that is hurting you – it is your own lie that you have been clinging to which hurts. Whenever you have to choose between a truth and a lie, be courageous and choose the truth, because that is the only way to live, the only way to know, the only way to be.

Enough for today.

the dimension of the mysterious

The first question:

Osho,
According to a very recent theory in astronomic physics, every atom which exists in the body or which builds up all material things around us comes out of a cosmic circle through which it must go at least twice. However, this fact doesn't help me to feel part of the cosmos. As a scientist, do I ever stand a chance of experiencing mystery?

Science is a demystification of existence. Hence, it is absolutely impossible to feel any sense of the mysterious through science; the very method of science prohibits it. It is just like somebody who is blind trying to see through the ears, or somebody who is deaf trying to listen to music through the eyes: the very method becomes the barrier.

Science has a definite methodology to it, and that makes it limited; it gives a demarcation, a definition. It is absolutely necessary for science to be defined, otherwise there would be no difference at all between science and meditation, between science and religious consciousness.

Science means being definite, being absolutely definite, about facts. If you are very definite about facts then you cannot feel mysterious – the more you are definite then the more mystery evaporates. Mystery needs a certain vagueness; mystery needs something undefined, undemarcated. Science is factual. Mystery is not factual; it is existential.

A fact is only a part of existence, a very small part, and science deals with the parts because it is easier to deal with the parts. They are small; you can analyze them. You are not overwhelmed by them; you can possess them in your hands. You can dissect them; you can label them, you can be absolutely certain about their qualities, quantities, possibilities – but in that very process mystery is being killed. Science murders mystery.

If you want to experience the mysterious you will have to enter from another door, from a totally different dimension. The dimension of the mind is the dimension of science, and the dimension of meditation is the dimension of the miraculous, the mysterious.

Meditation makes everything undefined. Meditation takes you into the unknown, uncharted. Meditation takes you slowly, slowly into a kind of dissolution where the observer and the observed become one. Now, that is not possible in science. The observer has to be the observer, and the observed has to be the observed, and a clear-cut distinction has to be maintained continuously. Not even for a single moment should you forget yourself, not even for a single moment should you become interested, dissolved, overwhelmed, passionate, loving toward the object of your inquiry. You have to be detached, you have to be very cold – cold, absolutely indifferent. And indifference kills mystery.

Between the world of meditation and the mind there is a bridge: that bridge is called the heart. The heart is just exactly between the two. Hence, the poet lives in a twilight land: something of him can be scientific and something of him can be mystic. That is the anxiety of the poet also, because he lives in two dimensions, diametrically opposite. Hence, poets tend to go mad, tend to commit suicide, are always known as a little bit crazy, outlandish. Something about them remains berserk for the simple reason that they are not settled anywhere. They are neither in the world of facts nor in the world of the existentials; they are in a limbo.

The poet can have a certain taste of the mysterious, but that too only rarely; it comes and goes. The mystic *lives* there; the poet only jumps once in a while and feels the joy of jumping beyond gravitation. But within a minute or within seconds he is back, crushed against the forces of gravitation.

Poetry is a kind of hopping. Once in awhile you are in the sky, for a moment you feel as if you have got wings, but only for a moment. Hence, the despair of the poet, because he falls again and again from his peaks. He gathers a few glimpses. The greatest poets, too, have been able to gather only a few glimpses of the beyond.

The mystic lives in the world of mystery. His approach is absolutely transcendental to science. He is neither in the mind nor in the heart, but in the beyond – he has transcended both.

If you really want the experience of the mysterious then you will have to open a new door in your being. I am not saying stop being a scientist; I am simply saying that science can remain a peripheral activity to you. When in the lab be a scientist, but when you come out of the lab forget all about science. Then listen to the birds, but not in a scientific way! Look at the flowers, but not in a scientific way, because when you look at a rose in a scientific way it is a totally different kind of thing that you are looking at. It is not the same rose that a poet experiences.

The experience does not depend on the object; the experience depends on the experiencer, on the quality of experiencing. When the scientist looks at the rose he thinks of colors, chemistry, physics, atoms, electrons, neutrons and whatnot…except beauty. Beauty does not come into his vision, and that's what the rose is.

To the poet, to the painter, it is a totally different experience: the rose is a manifestation of the unknown, of the transcendental, of the secret of life itself. It represents something of the divine; it brings into existence something of the sky, something of faraway stars. It grows on the earth; it is rooted in the earth, but it is not just part of the earth; it contains far more than that. It is greater than the sum total of its constituent parts. The scientist only comes to know it as a sum total of its constituent parts – there is nothing more to it – but the poet starts feeling something plus.

The moment you dissect the rose, the beauty disappears. The rose was only an opportunity for beauty to descend, a receptivity of the earth for the sky, a receptivity of the gross for the subtle. The poet feels that, but it is a feeling – it is not a thought.

So when you come out of your lab, forget all about atoms, forget all about the cosmos. Rather, start looking afresh, with a different vision – the vision of a child, the vision of a poet, the vision of a lover. When you look at the woman you love never think of her in terms of biology, otherwise you will miss the whole point. She is not biology, she has a being far greater than any biology can contain. When you kiss your woman don't think in terms of what is being transferred from lips to lips chemically, otherwise you will be disgusted! You won't see any poetry, you will be puzzled by what all these poets have been talking about. It is only an exchange of bacteria, germs, millions of germs, dangerous too. It can be a matter of life and death – beware!

When you are making love to your woman don't think in terms of hormones. Avoid that nonsense; otherwise the whole love act will be simply a mechanical phenomenon. You will be there and yet not there. You will be just an observer, not a participant. And the poet's whole secret is participation.

Looking at a flower, become the flower, dance around the flower, sing a song. The wind is cool and crisp; the sun is warm, and the flower is having its prime; the flower is dancing in the wind, rejoicing, singing a song, singing alleluia! Participate with it! Drop indifference, objectivity, detachment. Drop all your scientific attitudes. Become a little more fluid, more melting, more merging. Let the flower speak to your heart, let the flower enter your being. Invite him – he is a guest! And then you will have some taste of mystery.

This is the first step toward the mysterious, and the ultimate step is: if you can be a participant for a moment, you have known the key, the secret. Then become a participant in everything that you are doing. Walking, don't just do it mechanically, don't just go on watching it, *be* it. Dancing, don't do it technically; technique is irrelevant. You may be technically correct, and yet you will miss the whole joy of it. Dissolve yourself in the dance; become the dance; forget about the dancer.

When such deep unity starts happening in many, many phases of your life; when all around you, you start having such tremendous experiences of disappearance, egolessness, nothingness; when the flower is there and you are not, the rainbow is there and you are not; when the clouds are roaming in the sky within and without both, and you are not; when there is utter silence as far as you are concerned; when there is nobody in you, just a pure silence, a virgin silence, undistracted, undisturbed by logic, thought, emotion, feeling, that is the moment of meditation. Mind is gone, and when mind is gone mystery enters.

Mystery and mind cannot exist together; they are not, by their very nature, co-existent. Just like darkness and light: you cannot have both in your room. If you want darkness you have to extinguish the light; if you want light then you have to lose darkness. You can only have one, for the simple reason that the presence of light is the absence of darkness, the presence of darkness is the absence of light; they are not two things, in fact. The same phenomenon, present, is light; absent, is dark. Now you cannot manage both, to be together present and absent both.

Mind is the presence of the non-mysterious, the logical, and meditation is the presence of the mysterious, the miraculous.

Hence, move from the mind. Let art, poetry, painting, dancing become more important – they will bring you closer to meditation – and finally take the plunge. If you have tasted something of poetry you will gather courage enough to take the ultimate plunge.

To me religion consists of three layers; the first layer is of science. Just as your body consists of material, atomic constituents, religion consists first, the most peripheral part, of science. I am not against science; science is an absolute need, but it is only the peripheral phenomenon, the most superficial, the first concentric circle around your center. Then comes the second concentric circle which is deeper than science, that is of art, aesthetics. And then the third, that is meditation. And if you have entered these three concentric circles, slowly, slowly you will attain to the fourth.

The fourth in the East is called the *turiya*. We have not given it any name; we have simply given it a number, the fourth. Nothing can be said about it, that's why no word has been given to it. It is even beyond mystery. Meditation will take you into the mysterious, but there is still something more than that; that is inexpressible. Nothing can be said about it; nothing has ever been said about it; nothing will ever be said about it – but it has been experienced.

Only at that ultimate peak of experience, that ultimate ecstasy you will know what it is to be.

You ask me: "According to a very recent theory in astronomic physics, every atom which exists in the body or which builds up all material things around us comes out of a cosmic circle through which it must go at least twice." Whether it goes twice or thrice, how can it help you to feel that you are part of the cosmos? It may go thousands of times – it is irrelevant!

You say: "However, this fact doesn't help me to feel part of the cosmos." No fact can help you. You will have to travel the whole terrain from a totally different dimension.

You also ask: "Osho, as a scientist, do I ever stand a chance of experiencing mystery?" Not as a scientist; there is no chance. I cannot give you a wrong hope. As a scientist you have no chance of knowing the mysterious; but that does not mean that you have to stop being a scientist. That simply means that you let science be one of the aspects of your life. Why make it your whole life? Why become synonymous with it? It is perfectly good to use your logical mind, analytical mind – it is perfectly good, it is beneficial. The world needs technology, the world needs science, and you can be of immense service to humanity – but that is a totally different matter.

You should not think that this can be your whole life. Otherwise you will live only in the porch of the palace: and you will think that this is the palace, and you will suffer all kinds of things on the porch. Sometimes it will be too cold, and sometimes it will be too hot, and sometimes the rain will start coming in – it is only an open porch! And the palace is there, available; you could have entered the palace. I am not against the porch, remember, I am not telling you to demolish it. The porch is a necessity, but a porch is a porch. Pass through it, use it, but you have a beautiful palace – why not explore the whole palace of your being?

Explore poetry, explore music, explore dance, explore meditation, and finally and ultimately disappear into the fourth. Then, and only then, the goose is out!

The second question:

Osho,
When serious, sad people become enlightened, do they remain serious and sad or do they become funny like you?

Who has ever heard of serious people becoming enlightened? The serious person cannot become enlightened. Seriousness is a disease; it is the cancer of the soul. Seriousness is a wrong, utterly wrong approach to life. How can you come to truth through a wrong approach? The serious person is simply ill, pathological. Of course, for thousands of years serious people have dominated us because that is their only joy in life, there is no other joy for them – the joy of dominating.

There is a beautiful parable of Kahlil Gibran: Every day he goes for a morning walk, and he comes across a field where a false man, a scarecrow, has been placed. The false man has a purpose: he drives wild animals away, drives birds away from the crops.

One day Kahlil Gibran asks the false man, "You have been standing here year in, year out – you must be getting very tired, very bored?"

And the false man says, "No, I may look bored, I may look very serious, but I am enjoying my job."

Kahlil Gibran says, "What kind of enjoyment must you be having? I don't see anything here to enjoy for you"

He says, "The very joy of making people afraid gives such a thrill. Day in and day out, I am driving animals and birds crazy! They run away from me. I am the supreme being around here. I am the most powerful person. Everybody is afraid of me. Don't you think that's more than one can expect from life?"

The serious person has been doing that for centuries. In the name of politics, in the name of religion, in the name of education, in the name of morality, he has been torturing people; that is his only joy. He is basically a sadomasochist.

No sadomasochist can become enlightened; out of a hundred people that you thought became enlightened, ninety-nine point nine percent were not enlightened. It is just a traditional idea, and you go on carrying it. You have been told that this man is "enlightened." No criterion exists for you – how to judge him? Jesus is enlightened to the Christians; to the Jainas he is not; they have a different criterion. You will be surprised: to the Christians, Mahavira may not look enlightened at all; they have a different criterion.

Christians say Jesus never laughed in his whole life. This must be an absolute lie. I cannot believe it, that he never laughed; his whole life shows a different flavor. It is impossible to think that he never laughed, but Christians say that he never laughed. Why? – because an enlightened person has to be serious, very serious, burdened with all the problems of the world. He has come to solve all the problems, he has to come to save humanity. He is the savior, the messiah; he has to save you from your past sins, and future ones too. Naturally – he is carrying on his shoulders an Himalayan weight – how can he laugh? It is impossible.

The whole idea that somebody has to save you is ugly; the whole idea destroys your freedom. You are not even allowed to suffer for your own sins, somebody else has to suffer for them. Your whole responsibility for yourself is taken away.

That is not the vision of other traditions. For example, Buddha did not agree with it. He said, "Be a light unto yourself. Nobody else can save you." Hence, Buddha is not so serious; there is no need, there is no reason to be serious. He is freed from all his own problems, he is released. There is a subtle joy in him.

Christians will think that Buddha is selfish, that he is only thinking of himself. How can an enlightened person be selfish? Jesus is enlightened because he is thinking of all humanity.

Mahavira lived naked. That is the Jainas' concept of an enlightened man: that the enlightened person will renounce everything, he will live naked, and because he is completely free from all sins he cannot suffer. Jesus suffers much on the cross. Now, according to Jaina philosophy you suffer only because of your past bad karma. If Jesus had to suffer on the cross that simply shows that his past karma is still there – he has to pay for it; each act has to be paid for.

For Mahavira, they say that when Mahavira walks – and he walks naked, barefooted – if on the path there is a thorn, the thorn will immediately turn upside down, seeing that Mahavira is coming. Because Mahavira has no more sins left, the thorn cannot give any pain to Mahavira; what to say about crucifixion? But Mahavira is serious.

Krishna is not serious. Krishna is dancing, singing, playing on his flute.

When Bodhidharma became enlightened, for seven days he could not stop laughing. Asked why again and again, he only said this much: "I am laughing because the whole thing was ridiculous. The goose has always been out, and I was trying to bring it out of the bottle, and the bottle has never existed. The whole effort was sheer absurdity, ridiculous! I am laughing at myself and I am laughing at the whole world, because people are trying to do something which need not be done at all. People are trying hard, and the harder they try the more difficult it becomes. Their very effort is the barrier!"

How you are going to decide who is enlightened and who is not?

Just the other day I received a letter that said: "If you are really enlightened then you should hide yourself in the Himalayas, because the enlightened person always remains in hiding. They remain unknown, they remain unsung."

Now, if this man is right, then Mahavira, Buddha, Jesus, Krishna, Rama, Zarathustra, Mohammed – nobody is enlightened, because they are all well-known, world-known. They were not hiding in the Himalayas, they did not live anonymously; they did not die unsung.

Then one more question arises: how has this man come upon a few people who have lived hiding in the Himalayas, unsung, unknown, whom he thinks are the real enlightened people? How has he come to know about them? And if he knows, then they are not unknown – unless he is the only one who is allowed to know the secret! But these fools abound; they go on parading their own prejudices.

I will not tell you who is enlightened, who is not enlightened, but I will tell you of a simple phenomenon which you can understand and which can become a light for you. One thing is absolutely certain: that the sado-masochist cannot be enlightened. One who tortures himself and tortures others, enjoys torturing, cannot be enlightened.

Enlightenment is blissfulness; it cannot be serious. It can be sincere but not serious. It will be sheer joy! It will be pure ecstasy!

You ask me: "Osho, when serious, sad people become enlightened..." I have never heard of such a thing! And if you have heard about any sad and serious people becoming enlightened, then either they were not sad and serious or you have heard wrong. Serious and sad people become something else, they don't become enlightened. They become popes, Mother Teresas, Mahatma Gandhis, Morarji Desais, *shankaracharyas*, Ayatollah Khomaniacs, *imams*, priests. The churches, the synagogues, the temples, the mosques, the *gurudwaras* – they are full of these people; they are serious people. They gather around an enlightened person and they start destroying all that he has brought into being. They start creating a dead tradition – and the tradition has to be serious; the tradition cannot be nonserious.

The enlightened person is always joyous, but the tradition, the convention cannot be joyous. The whole structure of a tradition is basically political; it is to dominate, it is to oppress, it is to exploit. And you cannot exploit people playfully, you have to be very serious.

You have to make them so sad, so afraid of life itself; you have to create in their being so much trembling, that out of that fear they fall into your hands; they become objects of your manipulation.

A man like me cannot exploit you, because this whole place is more like a tavern than like a temple. It is more playful than serious. We are engaged in a beautiful game! The moment you think of it as a game, all seriousness disappears, things become lighter. You can walk in a dancing way; there is no weight on you.

The priests cannot do it; their whole prestige depends on their seriousness. The more serious they are, the more somber-looking, the more "holier-than-thou" they can pretend. They will do everything – they will fast...naturally when a person fasts he becomes serious, he cannot laugh. When you are hungry, starving, you cannot laugh – and you cannot allow anybody else to laugh either. It is not a laughing matter! You are starving, sacrificing, crucifying yourself, and people are laughing! It cannot be pardoned; it cannot be forgiven.

Naturally, when you go to a fasting person you become serious – you have to be serious. That is simply a mannerism. Now, a person who is distorting his body in every possible way, who is torturing his body in every possible way – how can you laugh around him? The very scene is sad; you feel burdened. It is very difficult to be with these so-called saints. That's why people just go to pay their respects and escape immediately, because to sit with them means they will burden you; they will create guilt in you.

For example, if they are fasting and you are well-fed, guilt is bound to be created. If they are standing on their heads and you are simply standing on your feet, you are doing something wrong. Naturally, you will think, "I am not yet a perfect man – this is the perfect man who is standing on his head." You see the sheer stupidity of it all? If God wanted you to stand on your head he would have managed!

If God had wanted homosexuality in the world, he would have created Adam and Bruce – it is so simple! Why bring Eve in? Unnecessary trouble! But these stupid people go on doing the unnatural, and their very unnatural approach to life naturally makes them serious. They are going against the current, they are exhausted, tired, bored, but their only joy is that they can bore you.

Moishe cannot decide about his son's future, so he goes to the rabbi and asks his advice.

The rabbi says, "That's very easy. We put the Talmud, the Torah and some money on the table, and let him choose. If he takes the Talmud he will become a rabbi. If he takes the Torah he will become a lawyer. If he takes the money he will become a shopkeeper."

Moishe agrees and they call his son. The son looks at all the things on the table and then takes them all.

Moishe is perplexed. "What will happen now?" he asks the rabbi.

"He will become a Catholic priest," replied the rabbi.

These sad people become Catholic priests, Hindu *shankaracharyas*, Mohammedan imams, and what-not. These serious people lose their humanity; they become parrots. But it pays. You need not have much intelligence to be a parrot; you need not have much courage to be a parrot; if you just have a little bit of memory, you can recite the Vedas, the Gita, the Koran, and you will be respected and honored. You are not doing anything creative, you are not adding to the beauty of the world, you are not contributing to the earth and its joys. On the contrary, you are destroying. But people are conditioned for thousands of years, and they go on doing things according to their conditioning. Parrots are worshipped.

A farmer owns a parrot who always screams, "Heil Hitler!"

One day the farmer gets fed up with the parrot and locks it in the hen house. The cock walks over to the parrot and asks, "Tell me, why did the farmer lock you in here?" The parrot remains silent.

"I will give you four of my hens if you tell me," continues the cock, but the parrot remains silent.

"Listen, if you tell me why he locked you in here, I'll give you ten of my hens."

The parrot turns around and screams, "Can't you leave me alone? I'm a political prisoner!"

These sad people, they either become priests or become politicians or become great pedagogues, professors, philosophers, theologians, but they never become enlightened. That much is absolutely certain – that cannot happen in the very nature of things.

To become enlightened one needs the lightness of the flower, the lightness of the feather, the multidimensional colors of the rainbow. One needs the joy of the birds in the morning; one needs the freedom of the clouds. One needs only one thing: a heart full of ecstasy – not ecstasy for something ultimate, not ecstasy for something in paradise, but ecstasy here and now, ecstasy this very moment. When your eyes are full of this very moment, when there is nothing else, no past, no future, when this moment pervades you so totally, so intensely, so passionately that nothing is left behind. Only these few people have become enlightened.

Hence I say, if you live in joyous ordinariness you are enlightened. There is no need for any spiritual nonsense, for any esoteric nonsense.

The toilet seat in the Rabinowitz's home was chipped. On his day off, Sidney promised to paint it. He had some nice bright green enamel in the garage and applied a fresh shiny coat.

Ethel went in with a magazine, sat down to meditate and read. When she tried to get up she found she was stuck! She yelled for Sid.

He tugged and tugged but could not pry her loose. Ethel, in desperation, cried, "So what are you standing there for! Call me a doctor! If plaster gets stuck, he at least knows how to remove it without tearing off the skin!"

Sidney dashed to the telephone and pleaded with the doctor to come right over. This was a real emergency! The doctor explained that he had an office full of patients and that he could not possibly get there for at least two hours.

Sid had a bright idea. He would unscrew the hinges and she could lie on the bed on her stomach and wait for the doctor. The two hours seemed like four but the doctor finally arrived.

Sidney directed him into the bedroom and pointing to his wife said, "Doc, ain't that something? What d'ya think of that?"

The doctor looked thoughtfully and declared, "Very nice...but why such a cheap frame?"

Life has to be taken hilariously! Life is so full of laughter; it is so ridiculous, it is so funny that unless your juices have gone completely dry you cannot be serious. I have looked around life in every possible way and it is always funny, whatever way you look at it! It gets funnier and funnier! It is such a beautiful gift of the beyond.

I am against all seriousness. My whole approach is that of humor, and the greatest religious quality is a sense of humor – not truth, not God, not virtue, but a sense of humor. If we can fill the whole earth with laughter, with dancing and singing – people singing and swinging! – if we can make the earth a carnival of joy, a festival of lights, we will have brought for the first time a true sense of religiousness to the earth.

The third question:

Osho,
Spiegel, the biggest news magazine in Germany, has finally started a series on you, your sannyasins and the ashram. The writer says many nice and incredible things about you and even compares you with the Pollack Pope. He says: "The masses who surrender to the charisma of John Paul II do nothing different than that which the Pune pilgrims do in their surrender to Osho. Only the churches and their sect experts cannot agree with that."
Do you feel offended or pleased by this statement?

I am amused! The Pollacks I have always loved. The Pope is secondary, the Pollack is the real thing. The Pollack is the elephant and the Pope is just the last part of the elephant, the tail part!

I am certainly not a pope, I cannot be – I am not that serious a man. I am not that religious either. I am very ordinary! To be a pope one needs to be very extraordinary. As far as charisma is concerned, I have none. I am just as ordinary as anybody else in the world. The whole idea of charisma is anti-human; it divides people. The whole strategy of creating charisma is nothing but the process of conditioning.

If you go to see a naked Jaina monk you will not see any charisma because you are not conditioned for that. You will simply see an ugly, disgusting-looking person, pale, ill, ill at ease, eyes almost dead, no intelligence on the face, the whole body shrunken. Yes, one thing will be big – the belly – because the Jaina monk eats only once a day so he has to eat too much. If you are not conditioned by Jaina ideas, the whole figure of a Jaina monk will appear like a caricature to you, a cartoon, but to the Jainas themselves there is charisma, great charisma.

Jaina monks, particularly the *digambara* Jaina monks who live naked, every year tear out their hair with their own hands. If you look at it, it will look insane, ugly, violent, but the Jainas watch with great respect – "Something of immense value is happening." The man is simply tearing out his hair! You must have seen your wife sometimes in anger, or if you go to a mad asylum you will find people tearing out their hair – just angry at themselves, violent anger at themselves, repressed anger and nothing else. But to the Jaina mind it is charismatic: "What sacrifice!"

If you go to a Christian church and see the cross, if you are conditioned by Christianity then you will not see that death is being worshipped – the cross represents death. There is every possibility if Jesus had not been crucified there would have been no Christianity at all. It is not Jesus who has dominated the Christian mind, it is the cross. Hence, I don't call Christianity, *Christianity*. I call it *Crossianity*! The cross simply symbolizes death, suicide; it is not a life-affirmative symbol. But to the Christian it symbolizes the great sacrifice of Jesus for the whole of humanity.

Charisma is created by a certain conditioning. The same Pope was not charismatic two years ago – suddenly he has become charismatic. What miracle has happened? Just because he is chosen to be the pope, he has been voted to be the pope, he has become charismatic. Now millions of people are impressed by him; nobody would have cared... The same man has been there for more than sixty years, and nobody had ever bothered about him. This is just a created illusion.

The same man, if he becomes the president of a country, starts having a charisma, and once he is no more a president he loses all charisma; then he is nobody.

When the revolution in Russia happened there was a very charismatic leader, Kerensky; he was the prime minister of Russia. In the revolution he escaped, and for fifty years nothing was heard about that charismatic leader. People had completely forgotten about him, and he was the most important man before Lenin in Russia; he had dominated the whole scene. After fifty years he died in New York as a grocer! When he died it was found that he is Kerensky and nobody else. For fifty years he was tending a grocery store and nobody ever thought of him as charismatic.

I am not charismatic, and I don't believe in all such nonsensical things. I exalt the simple, the unconditioned, the innocent, the ordinary, and I want all categories to be dissolved: the category of the sinner and the saint, the unholy and the holy, the profane and the sacred, the moral and the immoral. I want to dissolve *all* categories! Man is simply man.

So I would not like to be compared with the Pope. In fact, I don't like any comparison at all because comparison is basically a wrong approach. I am myself! I don't want to be compared even with Jesus; so what to say about the Pope. I don't want to be compared with Buddha, with Zarathustra, with Lao Tzu, because all comparison is basically wrong. Lao Tzu is Lao Tzu, I am who I am; there is no question of comparison.

How can you compare a rose bush with a cedar of Lebanon? There is no question of comparison. How can you compare the lotus with the marigold? In fact, two lotus flowers cannot even be compared with each other; they have their own uniqueness.

We have been living with this idea of comparison for centuries. We always compare, we always put people into categories, we always put people into boxes – who is who, what category one belongs in.

My whole effort here is to dissolve all categories and to declare the uniqueness of the individual. Never compare me with anybody else. I am simply myself. Good, bad, holy, unholy, whatsoever I am, I am simply myself. The very idea is disgusting, to be compared with anybody else. Existence never creates carbon copies, it always creates originals, and everybody comes with his own original face.

But Pollacks I love – that much I have to concede!

A Pollack walks into the office of a circus and offers to jump to the ground from ten meters up, head first, without a net. The manager does not believe this, so they go to the stage. The Pollack gets up to about ten meters, takes a deep breath and jumps head first. He crashes down on his head, lies still for a few moments and then gets up.

The manager is fascinated. "That's incredible!" he exclaims. "I will pay you one hundred dollars a night."

The Pollack shakes his head.

"Okay, okay, I will pay you three hundred dollars a night."

"No," replies the Pollack.

"I will pay you a thousand dollars!" says the manager.

"No," says the Pollack, "I've changed my mind – I don't want to jump anymore. I didn't know it would hurt so much."

A Pollack discovered that he had three balls. He was so anxious to tell it to someone that he stopped the first man he met on the road and asked him, "Do you want to bet that together we have five balls?"

He lost his bet...the other guy had only one ball!

The Pollack woman was dying. With her last breath she turned to her husband and asked, "Before I die, make love to me just one more time."

The Pollack husband answered, "How could you ask me to do such a thing? It will kill you!"

The wife pleaded, "Everyone is entitled to one last request before they die, you should grant me this last wish."

The Pollack replied, "Okay." He got into bed and made love to her. No sooner did he finish than she hopped out of bed, completely cured, ran downstairs and started to pluck a chicken, and yelled into the living room, where her children were sitting, that dinner would be ready in an hour.

The children were astounded and ran up the stairs to their father who was sitting in a chair and crying. They said, "Papa, why are you crying? It is a miracle! Mama is completely cured!"

He replied, "I know, but then I think what I could have done for Eleanor Roosevelt!"

The Pollack mind has its own way of working! It is the most intriguing mind in the world!

Spiegel has done one thing good : it has reminded me of the Pollack Pope.

The old Pollack general lived with his young wife in a lonely villa. They kept two guards in front of the house to protect them against intruders.

One night the guards saw that the lights in the general's bedroom were on for a very long time. Suspicious, they snuck up to the window and peeped in. The general's wife was lying on the bed naked, looking quite bored. The Pollack general, also naked, was anxiously walking around the room with a pistol in his hand.

Suddenly he stopped, looked down at his groin and shouted, "Stand up like a man or I will shoot!"

Do you remember the famous proverb: "The bread never falls but on its buttered side"?

However, there is a story of a Pollack man whose bread fell and landed buttered side up. He ran straightaway to the Pollack Pope to report this deviance from one of the basic rules of the universe.

At first the Pope would not believe him, but finally became convinced that it had happened. However, he did not feel immediately ready to deal with the question and asked for time. He studied hard the old scriptures about it, prayed to God and did all kinds of things to find an infallible answer.

After months of waiting he finally came up with an answer. He said to the Pollack man, "The bread must have been buttered on the wrong side."

You said, "*Spiegel*, the biggest news magazine in Germany, has finally started a series on you, your sannyasins and the ashram. The writer says many nice and incredible things about you and even compares you with the Pollack Pope. He says: 'The masses who surrender to the charisma of John Paul II do nothing different than that which the Pune pilgrims do in their surrender to Osho.'"

That is absolutely wrong. Because I am not here to help you to surrender to me. I don't want to stand between you and the whole. It is not a question of surrender. It is a question of surrender when you go to the Pope; here it is a love affair. There you surrender to the Pope because he represents God, represents the only begotten son of God, Jesus Christ. I don't represent anybody!

When you are with me you are living in a love affair; there is no question of surrender. You are simply learning ways of how to relate with existence. I am only an opportunity, a device, a catalytic agent at the most.

My sannyasins are not my followers. I'm not creating a church, I'm simply imparting what I have seen. I'm simply sharing my love, my joy, my experience. Those who are here are fellow travelers. You are not surrendered to me, but living with me. Slowly, slowly you will start enjoying a deep surrender with existence. That is a totally different matter; I have nothing to do with it. The credit will go to you, not to me. My presence can help only in one thing: to see the pattern of stupidity in which you are caught.

The Pope is simply enforcing the same stupid pattern in you.

For thousands of years people have been surrendering to these popes and priests and nothing has happened.

I am not a priest, and I am not interested in gathering crowds. I am not interested in creating a tradition; I am simply enjoying myself! Those who want to enjoy themselves, they are welcome. It is a place of joy. The very word *surrender* is irrelevant here! Nobody is surrendering to anybody else. You have to be yourself, authentically yourself, sincerely yourself, and then a miracle starts happening: the moment you discover your original face you enter into a communion with the whole.

Spiegel is not right in saying that the same thing is happening to Pune pilgrims; but when people come and just watch from the outside, these misunderstandings are bound to happen. They are just onlookers.

To understand what is going on here one has to be a participant, not just an observer. Only then will some taste on your tongue reveal the secret.

I have heard that every year as part of the splendid Easter ceremonials at St. Peter's in Rome, the Chief Rabbi of the city would enter the Basilica in solemn procession during High Mass and present the Pope with an ancient scroll. And every year the Pope would take this scroll, bow to the Rabbi and hand it back, whereupon the Rabbi would return the bow, turn and leave.

This mysterious rite had been going on for so many hundreds of years that no one could remember the origins of it nor what it symbolized. But the first Eastertide of Pope the Pollack's reign he decided to put an end to what had become a totally meaningless ritual, and so when the Chief Rabbi duly presented the scroll, His Holiness, to the consternation of the entire Curia, opened it up. It was a bill for the Last Supper.

The last question:

Osho,
I am going nuts! I keep laughing at a joke. I even woke up once laughing at it. And I don't even know what the joke is!

Then I will have to tell it again! In fact, there are four jokes.

Three I will tell you today and the fourth you have to discover – the *turiya*! I will give you forty-eight hours to discover it. If you cannot discover it then I will tell it too.

The first joke that I have been telling you in your *sushupti*, the dreamless sleep… Naturally, it is difficult to remember it. Yoga Lalita is my librarian, so I have to remind her continuously of jokes so she goes on collecting jokes for me. I never see her, I never go to the library, so the only way to convey the message is while she is asleep.

The first joke:

A minister, a priest and a rabbi were discussing how they divined what part of the collection money each retained for personal needs and what part was turned in to their respective institutions.

"I draw a line," said the minister, "on the floor. I toss all the money in the air – what lands to the right of the line I keep, to the left of the line is the Lord's."

The priest nodded, saying, "My system is essentially the same, only I use a circle. What lands inside is mine, outside is his."

The rabbi smiled and said, "I do the same thing. I toss all the money into the air and whatever God grabs is his!"

The second joke has been told to you in the state of *swapna*, the dream state. You may remember something of it – just a few fragments here and there.

The distraught young man was perched on the fortieth-floor ledge of a midtown hotel and threatening to jump. The closest the police could get was the roof of an adjacent building a few feet below. However, all pleas to the man to return to safety were of no avail. A priest from the nearest parish was summoned, and he hastened to the scene.

"Think, my son," he intoned to the would-be suicide. "Think of your mother and father who love you."

"Aw, they don't love me," the man replied. "I'm jumping!"

"No! Stop!" cried the priest. "Think of the woman who loves you!"

"Nobody loves me! I'm jumping!" came the response.

"But think," the priest implored, "think of Jesus and Mary and Joseph who love you!"

"Jesus, Mary and Joseph?" the man queried, "Who are they?"

At which point the cleric yelled back, "Jump, you Jew bastard, jump!"

The third has been told to you in *jagruti*, the so-called awakening state – which is not much of an awakening state. Maybe that's what goes on keeping you laughing.
You say: "I am going nuts! I keep laughing at a joke. I even woke up once laughing at it. And I don't even know what the joke is!"
This may be the joke:

The family managed to bring the patriarchal grandfather from Hungary, and he came to live with his daughter and her family. The old man was fascinated by New York and all it had to offer. One day, his grandson Yankel took him to the zoo in Central Park. Most of the animals were familiar to the old man. However, they came to the cage where the laughing hyena was confined and the old man became curious. "Yankel, in the old country I never heard of an animal that laughed."
Yankel noticed the keeper standing nearby and approached him. "My grandfather recently came here from Europe. He says they don't have laughing hyenas there. Could you tell me something about it so that I can, in turn, tell him about it?"
The keeper said, "Well, he eats once a day."
Yankel turned to his grandfather and in Yiddish translated, "Zayda, he eats once a day."
The keeper continued, "He takes a bath once a week."
"Zayda, he bathes once a week."
The old man listened intently.
The keeper added, "He mates once a year."
"Zayda, he mates once a year."
The old man nodded his head up and down and said thoughtfully, "All right, he eats once a day, he bathes once a week, but if he mates only once a year, why is he laughing?"

Enough for today.

rejoice to abandon!

The first question:

Osho,
Is it important to have some kind of attitude toward life?

The best way to miss life is to have a certain attitude toward it. Attitudes originate in the mind, and life is beyond mind. Attitudes are our fabrications, our prejudices, our inventions. Life is not our fabrication; on the contrary, we are just ripples in the lake of life.

What attitude can a ripple in the ocean have toward the ocean? What attitude can a grass blade have toward the earth, the moon, the sun, the stars? All attitudes are egoistic; all attitudes are stupid.

Life is not a philosophy; it is not a problem; it is a mystery. You have to live it not according to a certain pattern, not according to a conditioning – not what you have been told about it – you have to start afresh, from the very scratch.

Each human individual should think as if he is the first on the earth; he is the Adam or the Eve. Then you can open, you can open to infinite possibilities; then you will be vulnerable, available. The more vulnerable you are, the more available you are, the more is the possibility of life happening to you. Your attitudes function like barriers; then life never reaches you as it is – it has to fit your philosophy, religion, ideology; and in that very fitting, something dies in it. What you get out is a corpse: it may look like life but it is not.

That's what people have been doing down the ages. Hindus are living according to the Hindu attitude, Mohammedans according to the Mohammedan attitude, and Communists according to the Communist attitude. But remember a basic, fundamental truth: an attitude does not allow you to come into contact with life as it is; it distorts it, it interprets it.

There is an old Greek story:

A fanatic king had a beautiful golden bed, very precious, studded with thousands of diamonds, and whenever a guest would be in the palace he would offer the bed to the guest. But he had a certain attitude: the guest has to fit within the bed. If the guest was a little longer then the king would cut him to size. Of course, the bed was so valuable the bed could not be changed, but the guest was to be adjusted to the bed – as if the bed did not exist for the guests, but the guests exist for the bed!

It is very rare, almost impossible, to find a man to fit with a ready-made bed. The average person does not exist, remember; the average person is a fiction, and the bed was made for an average person. The king was a mathematician – great calculations had gone into it. He had counted the height of all the citizens of his capital, and then the heights were divided by the number of all the citizens; he had come up with a fixed average. Now, there were small children in the capital, young people, old people, pygmies, giants, but the average was a totally different phenomenon. There was not a single person in his whole capital who was really average. I have never come across the average person – the average person is a fiction.

So whosoever was going to be a guest was in trouble. If he was shorter than the bed, then the king had great wrestlers who would pull the man to size. That must have been the beginning of Rolfing! Ida Rolf must have learned it from that king. Of course, each guest died, but that was not the king's fault – he was doing everything with the best of intentions in the world!

When you have a certain attitude toward life, you will miss life itself. Life is vast, uncontainable in any attitude; impossible to put into a certain definition. Your attitude may cover a certain aspect, but it will be only an aspect. The tendency of the mind is to proclaim its aspect as the whole, and the moment an aspect is claimed as the whole you have missed the very connection with life. Then you will live surrounded by your attitude in a kind of cocoon, encapsulated, and you will be miserable. Then all your so-called religions will be very happy because that's what they have been telling to you: that life is misery.

Buddha says birth is misery, youth is misery, old age is misery, death is misery – the whole of life is nothing but a long, long tragedy. If you start with attitudes you will find Buddha absolutely correct; you will be a proof.

But I want to tell you that life is not misery; I don't agree with Buddha at all. Life becomes a misery, but that is your doing; otherwise life is eternal joy. To know that eternal joy you have to come open-hearted, open-handed.

Don't approach life with your fists closed, clenched. Open your hands. Go into life with immense innocence. Attitudes are cunning: you have already decided without tasting, without experiencing, without living. You have already arrived at certain conclusions, and of course if those conclusions are there already in you *a priori*, you will find them confirmed by life. Not that life confirms them, but your whole mind will try to find ways and means, arguments, data to support them.

Mind is like a sponge: it goes on sucking. It is a parasite. Once there is the center of a certain *a priori* conclusion, then that center starts becoming crystallized.

A man came to me who had been working for years from a certain hypothesis. In many countries of the world: particularly in the West, and more particularly in America, the number thirteen is not thought to be good. There are hotels in America where the thirteenth floor does not exist; from the twelfth floor you come to the fourteenth. The number thirteen is avoided; no room has the number thirteen; from the twelfth you immediately come to the fourteenth, because nobody wants to live in the thirteenth room or on the thirteenth floor. A great fear – the idea that the number thirteen has something evil in it.

This man had worked and collected all kinds of data, and he had collected a really huge, mountainous support – how many accidents happen on the thirteenth of every month, how many people die on the thirteenth, how many people commit suicide, how many people murder, how many people go mad.

He showed his great thesis to me, and he said, "What do you say?"

I said, "You do one more thing. You have put so much energy into this, now try one more thing. Now find out what happens on the twelfth! You will come to the same data, because on the twelfth people also go mad, commit suicide, murder, rob. Everything happens every day, but if you have a certain attitude, fixed, then you will choose your data according to that attitude. Of course when you have so much information and such an argument you feel certain that your attitude is right."

I teach you a life without any attitudes. This is one of the fundamentals of my experience: if you really want to know that which is, then drop all philosophy, all "ism." Then go open-handed, utterly naked into the sun to see what it is.

In the past it was thought that our senses are doors; reality reaches through our senses into our innermost being. Now the latest research shows something else: our senses are not just doors, they are guards also. Only two percent of outside information is allowed to pass in, ninety-eight percent stays outside. Anything that goes against your idea of life is prevented from entering, and only two percent filters in.

To live a life of only two percent is not to live at all. When one can live a hundred percent, why decide to live for only two percent?

You ask me: "Is it important to have some kind of attitude toward life?" Not only is it not important, it is dangerous to have any attitude toward life. Why not allow life to have its dance, its song, without any expectations? Why can't we live without expectations? Why can't we see that which is, in its purity? Why should we impose ourselves upon it? And nobody is going to be the loser. If you impose expectations upon life you are the only loser.

From London comes the story of the three professors of literature who, while returning from lunch, encountered several ladies of pleasure who were patrolling the street, *en masse*.

"What might one call such a congregation?" mused the first professor, a Shakespearean specialist. "A flourish of strumpets?"

The second professor, being an authority on the novels of Anthony Trollope, naturally contributed, "A chapter of trollops."

But the best description came from the youngest and the least specialized of the professors. He called the ladies "an anthology of pros."

It is better not to label life, it is better not to give it a structure, it is better to leave it open-ended, it is better not to categorize it, not to label it. You will have a more beautiful experience of things; you will have a more cosmic experience of things, because things are not really divided. Existence is one orgasmic whole; it is one organic unity. The smallest blade of grass, the smallest leaf in a poor tree is as significant as the biggest star. The smallest thing is also the biggest because it is all oneness; it is one spectrum. The moment you start dividing you start creating arbitrary lines, definitions, and that's the way one goes on missing life and the mystery of it.

We all have attitudes, that is our anguish; we all look from certain standpoints. Hence our life becomes poor, because every aspect at the most can be only one-dimensional, and life is multi-dimensional. You have to be more liquid, more fluid, more melting and merging; you are not to be an observer. There is nothing to be solved! Don't take life as a problem, it is a tremendously beautiful mystery. Drink of it – it is pure wine! Be a drunkard with it!

A successful couturier had finally found the girl of his dreams and he made preparations for a wedding the garment district would never forget. His own designers prepared a wedding gown for the bride, of the finest imported silks and satins, and his own marital raiment was truly a sight to behold.

The affair was nothing less than breathtaking; no expense had been spared. Then, as the newlyweds were about to embark on their honeymoon trip to Canada, an urgent message arrived in the form of a telegram.

"It is from my partner," the groom explained. "Urgent business. I will have to attend to it immediately."

"But what about our honeymoon?" the bride asked tearfully.

"Business comes first," he said. "But you go ahead. I will catch a later plane and be there by tonight."

"But what if you can't make it by tonight?" she moaned.

"Then," he blustered, "start without me."

A businessman has his own philosophy, his own attitudes. The scientist has his own attitudes. Everybody is living in a small prison of his own attitudes.

My effort here is to bring you out of your imprisonment. Hence I don't teach you any doctrine, I don't give you any dogma, I don't give you any creed to live by. I am simply trying to help you to be unburdened of all the nonsense which has been imposed upon you for centuries. If you can put aside the mountainous weight of the past, if you can start living as if you are the first man, only then there is a possibility that you may come to know what godliness is, what freedom is, what joy is. Otherwise, misery is going to be your lot, and naturally, sooner or later, you will agree with the pessimist attitude of Buddha: that all is suffering, all is pain.

I absolutely deny it, because my own experience is just the opposite: all is bliss, all is benediction. But it depends on you, how you approach life: guarded, with certain spectacles on your eyes, or unguarded, in deep trust, in love.

The second question:

Osho,
In the past all famous artists have been well-known for their bohemian style of life. Please can you say something about creativity and discipline?

The bohemian life is the only life worth living! All other kinds of lives are only lukewarm; they are more ways of committing slow suicide than ways of living life passionately and intensely. In the past it was inevitable that the artist has to live in rebellion, because creativity is the greatest rebellion in existence. If you want to create you have to get rid of all conditioning, otherwise your creativity will be nothing but copying – it will be just a carbon copy. You can be creative only if you are an individual; you cannot create as part of the mob psychology. The mob psychology is uncreative: one lives a life of drag – one knows no dance, no song, no joy, it is mechanical.

Of course, there are a few things you will get from the society if you are only mechanical: you will get respectability, you will get honors. Universities will confer D.Litt's on you; countries will give you gold medals; you may finally become a Nobel laureate – but this whole thing is ugly.

A real man of genius will discard all this nonsense, because this is bribery. Giving a Nobel Prize to a person simply means that your services to the establishment have been respected, that you are honored because you have been a good slave, obedient, that you have not gone astray, that you have followed the well-trodden path.

A creator cannot follow the well-trodden path; he has to search his own way; he has to inquire into the jungles of life, he has to go alone, he has to be a dropout from the mob mind, from the collective psychology. The collective mind is the lowest mind in the world; even the so-called idiots are a little bit superior to the collective idiocy. And the collectivity has its own bribes: it respects people, honors people, if they go on insisting that the way of the collective mind is the only right way.

It was out of sheer necessity that in the past the creators of all kinds – the painters, the dancers, the musicians, the poets, the sculptors – had to renounce respectability. They had to live a kind of bohemian life, the life of a vagabond; that was the only possibility for them to be creative. This need not be so in the future. If you understand me, if you feel what I am saying has a truth in it, then in the future everybody should live individually, and there will be no need for a bohemian life. The bohemian life is a by-product of a fixed, orthodox, conventional, respectable life.

My effort is to destroy the collective mind and to make each individual free to be himself or herself. Then there is no problem; then you can live as you want to live. In fact, humanity will be really born only the day the individual is respected in his rebellion. Humanity is still not born; it is still in the womb. What you see as humanity is only a very hocus-pocus phenomenon. Unless we give individual freedom to each person, absolute freedom to each person to be himself, to exist in his own way... Of course, he has to not interfere with anybody else – that is part of freedom. Nobody should interfere with anybody else.

In the past everybody was poking his nose into everybody else's affairs – even into things which are absolutely private, which have nothing to do with the society. For example, you fall in love with a woman – what has that got to do with the society? It is purely a personal phenomenon; it is not of the marketplace. If two persons are agreeing to commune in love, the society should not come into it, but the society comes in with all its paraphernalia, in direct ways, in indirect ways. The policeman will stand between the lovers; the magistrate will stand between the lovers; and if that is not enough then the societies have created a super-policeman, a God, who will take care of you.

The idea of the God is that of a peeping tom who does not even allow you privacy in your bathroom, who goes on looking through the keyhole, watching what you are doing. This is ugly. All the religions of the world say God continuously watches you – this is ugly. What kind of God is this? Has he got no other business than watching everybody, following everybody? Seems to be the supreme-most detective!

Humanity needs a new soil – the soil of freedom. Bohemianism was a reaction, a necessary reaction, but if my vision succeeds then there will be no bohemianism because there will be no so-called collective mind trying to dominate people. Then everybody will be at ease with himself. Of course, you are not to interfere with anybody else, but as far as your life is concerned you have to live it on your own terms. Only then there is creativity. Creativity is the fragrance of individual freedom.

You ask me, "Please can You say something about creativity and discipline?" *Discipline* is a beautiful word, but it has been misused as all other beautiful words have been misused in the past. The word *discipline* comes from the same root as the word *disciple*; the root meaning of the word is "a process of learning." One who is ready to learn is a disciple, and the process of being ready to learn is discipline.

The knowledgeable person is never ready to learn, because he already thinks he knows; he is very much centered in his so-called knowledge. His knowledge is nothing but nourishment for his ego. He cannot be a disciple; he cannot be in true discipline.

Socrates says, "I know only one thing – that I know nothing." That is the beginning of discipline. When you don't know anything, of course, a great longing to inquire, explore, investigate arises. The moment you start learning, another factor follows inevitably: whatsoever you have learned has to be dropped continuously, otherwise it will become knowledge and knowledge will prevent further learning.

The real man of discipline never accumulates; each moment he dies to whatsoever he has come to know and again becomes ignorant.

That ignorance is really luminous. I agree with Dionysus when he calls ignorance luminous. It is one of the most beautiful experiences in existence to be in a state of luminous not-knowing. When you are in that state of not-knowing you are open; there is no barrier, you are ready to explore. The Hindus cannot do it – they are already knowledgeable. The Mohammedans cannot do it, the Christians cannot do it. My sannyasins *can* do it, for the simple reason that I am not imparting knowledge; on the contrary, I am destroying your knowledge.

Hence it happens every day...every day I receive many letters, many questions. One friend has come from the West. He says, for three, four years he has been reading my books, and he was so excited. He was in such love with me that he wanted to come somehow as quickly as possible. Now he has managed to come, but here he feels frustrated. He was four years in deep love with me, and now he says, "I cannot say the same, because you are so shocking to me. You irritate me, you annoy me; you go on hammering on my cherished ideas."

It is easy to read a book because the book is in your hands, *I* am not in your hands! You can interpret the book according to your ideas, you cannot interpret me according to your ideas – I will make so much trouble for you! He was not in love with me, he was in love with his own ideas, but because he was finding support from my books he lived in an illusion.

With me illusions are bound to be shattered. I am here to shatter all illusions. Yes, it will irritate you, it will annoy you – that's my very way of functioning and working. I will sabotage you from your very roots! Unless you are totally destroyed as a mind, there is no hope for you.

Discipline has been misinterpreted. People have been telling others to discipline their life, to do this, not to do that. Thousands of should's and should-not's have been imposed on man, and when a man lives with thousands of should's and should-not's he cannot be creative. He is a prisoner; everywhere he will come across a wall.

The creative person has to dissolve all should's and should-not's. He needs freedom and space, vast space. He needs the whole sky and all the stars – only then his innermost spontaneity can start growing.

So remember, my meaning of discipline is not that of the Ten Commandments. I am not giving you any discipline; I am simply giving you an insight of how to remain in learning and never become knowledgeable. Your discipline has to come from your very heart, it has to be *yours* – and there is a great difference. When somebody else gives you the discipline it can never fit you; it will be wearing somebody else's clothes. Either they will be too loose or too tight, and you will always feel a little bit silly within them.

Mohammed has given a discipline to the Mohammedans: it may have been good for him, himself, but it cannot be good for anybody else. Buddha has given a discipline to millions of Buddhists: it may have been good for him, himself, but it cannot be good for everybody else. A discipline is an individual phenomenon; whenever you borrow it you start living according to set principles, dead principles. And life is never dead, life is constantly changing each moment. Life is a flux.

Heraclitus is right: you cannot step in the same river twice. In fact, I myself would like to say you cannot step in the same river even once – the river is so fast moving! One has to be alert, watchful, to each situation and its nuances, and one has to respond to the situation according to the moment, not according to any ready-made answers given by others.

Do you see the stupidity of humanity? Five thousand years ago, Manu gave a discipline for the Hindus, and they are still following it. Three thousand years ago Moses gave a discipline to the Jews, and they are still following it. Five thousand years ago Adinatha gave his discipline to the Jainas, and they are still following it. The whole world is being driven crazy by these disciplines! They are out of date, they should have been buried long, long ago. You are carrying corpses, and those corpses are stinking. And when you live surrounded by corpses, what kind of life can you have?

I teach you the moment, and the freedom of the moment, and the responsibility of the moment. One thing may be right this moment and may become wrong the next moment. Don't try to be consistent, otherwise you will be dead. Only dead people are consistent. Try to be alive, with all its inconsistencies, and live each moment without any reference to the past, without any reference to the future either. Live the moment in the context of the moment, and your response will be total. And that totality has beauty, and that totality is creativity. Then whatsoever you do will have a beauty of its own.

The third question:

Osho,
I have discovered that I am just bored with myself and I feel no

juice. You have said to accept ourselves, whatever we are. I am not able to accept life – knowing that I am missing something of joy inside. What to do?

We hear there is a new type of tranquilizer that does not relax you – just makes you dig being tense.

You try it! Try it and try it and try it again – be an American! – but not more than three times. Try it, try it, and try it again, and then stop because there is no point in being silly.

You say: "I have discovered that I am just bored with myself…"

This is a great discovery. Yes, I mean it! Very few people are aware that they are bored, and they *are* bored, utterly bored. Everybody else knows except themselves. To know that one is bored is a great beginning; now a few implications have to be understood.

Man is the only animal who feels boredom; it is a great prerogative, it is part of the dignity of human beings. Have you seen any buffalo bored, any donkey bored? They are not bored. Boredom simply means that the way you are living is wrong; hence it can become a great event, the understanding that "I am bored and something has to be done, some transformation is needed." So don't think that it is bad that you are feeling bored – it is a good sign, a good beginning, a very auspicious beginning. But don't stop there.

Why does one feel bored? One feels bored because one has been living in dead patterns given to you by others. Renounce those patterns, come out of those patterns! Start living on your own.

Only the authentic person is not bored, the pseudo person is bound to be bored. The Christian will be bored, the Jaina will be bored, the Parsi will be bored, the Communist will be bored, because they are dividing their life into two parts. Their real life remains repressed, and they start pretending an unreal life. It is unreal life that creates boredom. If you are doing the thing you are meant to do you will never be bored.

The day I left my home for the university my parents – my father, my family people – all wanted me to become a scientist. There was much more future for a scientist – or at least a doctor, or an engineer. I refused absolutely. I said, "I'm going to do what I want to do, because I don't want to live a bored life. As a scientist I may succeed – I may have respectability, money, power, prestige – but deep down I will remain bored because that is not what I ever wanted to do."

They were shocked because they could not see any prospects in studying philosophy; philosophy is the poorest subject in the universities. Reluctantly they agreed, knowing that I was wasting my future, but finally they recognized that they were wrong.

It is not a question of money, power and prestige; it is a question of what intrinsically you want to do. Do it, irrespective of the results, and your boredom will disappear. You must be following others' ideas, you must be doing things in a right way, you must be doing things as they should be done. These are the foundation-stones of boredom.

The whole of humanity is bored because the person who would have been a mystic is a mathematician, the person who would have been a mathematician is a politician, the person who would have been a poet is a businessman. Everybody is some-where else; nobody is where he should be. One has to risk. Boredom can disappear in a single moment if you are ready to risk.

You ask me: "I have discovered that I am just bored with myself..." You are bored with yourself because you have not been sincere with yourself, you have not been honest with yourself. You have not been respectful of your own being.

You say: "I feel no juice." Where can you feel juice from? Juice flows only when you are doing the thing that you wanted to do, whatsoever it is.

Vincent van Gogh was immensely happy just painting. Not a single painting was sold; nobody ever appreciated him, and he was dying. He was hungry because his brother was giving him only a small amount of money so that he could at least manage to survive. Four days he fasted and three days in the week he would eat. He had to fast for those four days because where was he going to get his canvases and paints and brushes from? But he was immensely happy – juices were flowing.

He died when he was only thirty-three. He committed suicide – but his suicide is far better than your so-called life, because he committed suicide only when he had painted the thing that he wanted to paint.

The day he finished a painting of a sunset, which was his longest desire, he wrote a letter saying, "My work is done, I am fulfilled. I am leaving this world immensely contented." He committed suicide, but I will not call it suicide. He lived totally, he burned his life's candle from both ends together, in tremendous intensity.

You may live a hundred years, but your life will be just a dry bone, a weight, a dead weight.

You say: "Osho, you have said to accept ourselves, whatever we are. I am not able to accept life – knowing that I am missing something of joy inside." When I say accept yourself, I am not saying accept your pattern of life – don't misunderstand me. When I say accept yourself, I am saying reject everything else – accept yourself. But you must have interpreted this in your own way. That's how things go...

The Martian landed his saucer in Manhattan and, immediately upon emerging, was approached by a panhandler. "Mister," said the man, "can I have a dime?"

The Martian asked, "What is a dime?"

The panhandler thought a minute, then said, "You're right. Can I have a quarter?"

I have not said what you have understood. Reject all that has been imposed on you – I am not saying to accept it. Accept your innermost core which you have brought from the beyond, and then you will not feel that you are missing something. The moment you accept yourself without any conditions, suddenly an outburst of joy happens. Juices start flowing, life really becomes ecstatic.

A certain young man's friends thought he was dead, but he was only in a state of coma. When, just in time to avoid being buried, he showed signs of life, he was asked how it felt to be dead.

"Dead!" he exclaimed. "I was not dead. I knew all the time what was going on. And I knew I was not dead, too, because my feet were cold and I was hungry."

"But how did that fact make you think you were still alive?" asked one of the curious.

"Well, I knew that if I was in heaven I would not be hungry, and if I was in the other place my feet would not be cold."

One thing is certain – that you are still not dead: you are hungry, your feet are cold. Just get up and do a little jogging!

A poor man, lacking education and all the social graces, fell in love with the daughter of a millionaire. She invited him home to meet her parents at their elegant mansion. The man was intimidated by the rich furnishings, the servants and all the other signs of wealth, but somehow he managed to appear relaxed – until it came to dinner time. Seated at the massive dinner table, mellow with the effects of wine, he farted loudly.

The girl's father looked up and stared at his dog which was lying at the poor man's feet. "Rover!" he said in a menacing tone.

The poor man was relieved that the blame had been put on the dog, and so a few minutes later he farted again.

His host looked at the dog and again said, "Rover!" in a louder voice.

A few minutes later he farted a third time. The rich man's face wrinkled in rage. He bellowed, "Rover, get the hell out of here before he shits all over you!"

There is still time – get out of the imprisonment in which you have lived up to now! It needs only a little courage, just a little courage of the gambler. There is nothing to lose, remember. You can only lose your chains – you can lose your boredom, you can lose this constant feeling inside you that something is missing. What else there is to lose? Get out of the rut, and accept your own being – against Moses, Jesus, Buddha, Mahavira, Krishna. Accept yourself. Your responsibility is not toward Buddha or Zarathustra or Kabir or Nanak; your responsibility is only toward you.

Be responsible – and when I use the word *responsible*, please remember, don't misinterpret. I am not talking about duties, responsibilities, I am simply using the word in the literal sense: respond to reality, be response-able.

You must have lived an irresponsible life, fulfilling all kinds of responsibilities which others are expecting you to. What is there to lose? You are bored – this is a good situation – you are missing the juice; what more do you need to get out of the prison? Jump out of it, don't look back!

They say: Think twice before you jump. I say: Jump first and then think as much as you want!

The fourth question:

Osho,

Can a madman become a buddha?

Only a madman can become a buddha! The so-called sane people at the most can become Buddhists but not buddhas, they can become Christians but not Christs. Only a madman...

My invitation is for the mad people of the world. I am a madman's guide to enlightenment!

A group of philosophers from the Russian prison decided to escape. They had a duplicate key, so they waited for night to make their escape. At midnight one of them went to open the door, but came back after a few minutes with a long sad face.

"What happened?" asked all the others.

"Well, our plan is useless. We can't escape – the crazy night-watchman has forgotten to close the door and I can't use the key!"

Philosophers cannot become buddhas! It needs guts to become a buddha.

Jesus was hanging on the cross when a philosopher passed by. He stopped, looked at Jesus and asked, "What are you doing up there?"

Jesus nodded his head to the left and right and said, "I'm hanging out with friends!"

The philosopher continued, "Well, if you want, I could get a ladder and take you down."

"I would appreciate that," Jesus replied.

Half an hour later the philosopher came back with a ladder, climbed up to the cross, screwed the nails out of the right hand, then out of the left hand.

Jesus fell headlong, screaming, "You idiot! Next time start with the feet!"

The last question:

Osho,
I want to get lost utterly and ultimately into absolute love. What should I do?

The very idea of getting lost utterly, ultimately, absolutely, is demanding too much. Be a little more human, don't aspire to the impossible. The impossible has been driving people to unnecessary hysteria, and we have been burdened with impossible values for centuries. We have learned these words and we go on repeating these words, parrot-like, without even taking in the significance.

Be human, don't aspire for perfection in any way because all perfectionism is neurosis. Be human and accept all the frailties and limitations of human beings. Why should you want to be lost utterly? For what? What you are going to gain out of it? If it *can* be managed – it is good that it cannot be managed... For argument's sake I am saying if it can be managed, you will come again saying, "Now I am feeling very lonely, utterly lost, absolutely lost, ultimately lost!" You will start hankering to go back, to have a little more spice of life.

It is good to meet and merge, but why make it something ultimate? Why bring such meaningless words? Is it not enough to melt for a moment and then be back home? Then there is a rhythm: you melt, you enjoy the melting, then again you are back. It creates a rhythm, and rhythm is always richer. If you are simply dissolved forever there will be no rhythm, no music, no dance. It will be really death, not life.

My whole approach is to teach you to be human. For centuries you have been told to be super-human. I rejoice in your humanness. To me, humanness is synonymous with godliness.

It is perfectly beautiful to be lost once in a while and found again, so that you can lose yourself again. Create a rhythm of getting lost, of finding oneself again. Life is a music, and the music is possible only if both things continue, otherwise it will be monotonous.

I cannot help you in getting lost absolutely, ultimately, utterly. I love the moment, I love the immediacy of the moment. I am very averse to words like *ultimate*; they are faraway words, they don't have much meaning in them; they are pretentious words.

The absolute is not of any significance; a rose flower is of far more significance. It is not absolute: in the morning it grows, by the evening it is gone. That's its beauty – it is momentary. It is a miracle! The ultimate rose will be synthetic, plastic, it will be there forever – but because it will not be able to die it will not be alive either.

In life, you have to learn this synchronicity of losing and then coming back to yourself and losing again – the closeness of love and the distance. Each distance in love again creates a longing to be close. If you are stuck together and you cannot separate, your love-life will become a nightmare.

Meditate over this story; it is a beautiful parable. Only I can say it is a parable.

Rosalie Mazzolli, nee Adelstein, had married a midget. For a while they were getting along all right, but one day Rosalie showed up in domestic relations court and demanded she be granted divorce from little Harry.

"Surely, Mrs. Mazolli, you knew your husband was a midget when you married him?" questioned the judge. "Why are you now desirous of leaving him? Didn't you anticipate the problems this marriage would encounter?"

"Oh, Your Honor," sobbed Rosalie, "how was I to know? Everything is wonderful, except for sex."

"Sex?" repeated the judge. "What has his being a midget got to do with sex?"

"Well," she continued tearfully, "when we're nose to nose his toes are in it; when we're toes to nose, his nose is in it, and when he's in it he disappears altogether. And oh, Your Honor, I get so lonely!"

There is no need to be utterly, ultimately, absolutely lost. Be relaxed – once in a while get lost and that is good. Lose yourself and find yourself again and again. This is a beautiful drama, this existence, of losing and finding. And drop all these words *ultimate*, *absolute*, *perfect*; these are all just words, inventions of the philosophers. Life is immediate; life is always now and here. Live it with all the frailty of a human being, with all the frailty of a rose flower, and you will come to know the greatest splendor *in the moment* – not in eternity. It is always now and it is always here! Don't condemn the momentary – rejoice in it, rejoice to abandon.

Enough for today.

CHAPTER 10

dissolve in my people

The first question:

Osho,
I frequently hear a question being asked about the ashram...there
is so much vitality here now and so much creativity with all these
shows and music and fashions and crafts, as well as events
happening abroad, that people are wondering what will happen
when you are gone.
When you leave your body will the ashram become a dead
institution, and will you just become deified and forgotten?

M y concern is the immediate, this moment. Beyond this moment
nothing exists. The only time that is existential is now, and the
only space that matters is here. So I don't care what happens
in the future – neither the past nor the future have any validity.

But that is the way of the mind: the mind can only think in terms
of past and future; the mind cannot experience the present; it devi-
ates from the present continuously. The mind is like a pendulum: it
moves to the left, far left, or to the right, far right. Either it is leftist or
rightist – and my whole approach is to be exactly in the middle.

The word for the middle which Gautama the Buddha used is very beautiful: he called it *majjim nikaya*, "the way of the exact middle." If you can keep the pendulum in the middle, the clock stops. The clock represents the mind – not only literally, not only as a metaphor; mind *is* time. Time consists of two tenses, not three. The present is not part of time; past is time, future is time. The present is the penetration of the beyond into the world of time.

You can think of time as a horizontal line. *A* is being followed by *b*, *b* is followed by *c*, *c* is followed by *d*, so on and so forth: it is a linear procession. Existence is not horizontal, existence is vertical. Existence does not move in a line – from *a* to *b*, from *b* to *c* – existence moves in intensity: from *a* to a deeper *a*, from the deeper *a* to even deeper *a*. It is diving into the moment.

Time conceived as past and future is the language of the mind – and the mind can only create problems – it knows no solutions. All the problems that humanity is burdened with are mind inventions. Existence is a mystery, not a problem. It has not to be solved, it has to be lived.

I am living my moment. I don't care a bit what happens later on. It may look to you very irresponsible because my criterion of responsibility is diametrically opposite to the so-called people's idea of responsibility. I am responsible to the moment, to existence – and responsible not in the sense of being dutiful to it, but responsible in the sense that I respond totally, spontaneously. Whatsoever the situation is, I am utterly in tune with it. While I am alive I am alive, when I am dead I am dead. I don't see any question at all.

But I can understand your question. You say: "I frequently hear a question being asked about the ashram…"

The people who are asking you are dead, otherwise why should they be worried about the future? They don't come to the ashram, they don't come to me, they have no participation with all that is going on here. They are concerned about the future! They are showing much worry about the future – what will happen? The question is: what is happening?

The people who are asking such questions are stupid, too. Are they going to live forever? They are worried about me and my work as if they are going to be here forever. I am here for the moment; you are here for the moment. If a meeting is possible, something of tremendous beauty can happen. But these fools go on thinking in such cunning ways that they not only deceive others, they manage even to deceive themselves. Right now they are condemning me, right now they are criticizing me, and still they are showing great love – what will happen when I am no longer here?

The moment I die, the whole world dies for me; then whatsoever happens, happens. I have not taken the responsibility for the whole of existence. Who can take it? There have been people who have tried it and they have all utterly failed.

For example, Gautama the Buddha – one of the most beautiful men who has ever walked on the earth – was very much concerned that no religion should arise when he has left the world, that he should not be worshipped, that his statues should not be made. He emphasized again and again his whole life, forty-two years of constant sermonizing to people, saying, "There is no need to worship me," and it brought just the opposite result. The more he emphasized "Don't worship me," the more people felt "This is the man to be worshipped."

This is the law of reverse effect. More statues of Buddha have been made in the world than of anybody else, and he was against statues. So many statues have been made of Buddha that in Urdu, Arabic, and other Mohammedan languages, the very word *buddha* has become synonymous with statue, with a little change: *budh*. *Budh* means the statue, but *budh* comes from *buddha*. Thousands of statues...and the man was emphasizing "Don't make statues of me!"

In fact, there was no need to emphasize it. The very emphasis was wrong. Why should he be concerned about the future? When you are no more there, the very desire to control the future according to your ideas is political. People are trying to control humanity when they are alive and they go on insisting that they would like to control humanity even when they are gone.

I am not controlling anybody; I am not a politician. I am not interested at all that anybody should be controlled by me today or tomorrow.

Now, the same kind of thing is being done by J. Krishnamurti: continuously emphasizing for fifty years: "I am not your guru." But for fifty years if you are not the guru, why go on emphasizing it? There must be something in it. He is afraid; there is the fear: he knows that he will be worshipped; he knows that there are already people who think of him as their real guru. The more he freaks out, the more those fools think, "This is the real guru! Look how humble he is – no pretensions, no desire, no ambition to be holier-than-thou." Ponder over it.

Krishnamurti is doing again the same thing that Buddha did. He is not original at all about it; it is an old game. In fact, people's minds work in a strange way. God said to Adam and Eve, "Don't eat the fruit of the tree of knowledge," and they ate it. The moment you say no, something deep in the heart of man starts becoming interested; a great curiosity arises. So I am not saying to anybody, "Please don't worship me."

When I am not there, what can I do? Fools are fools. Whether they worship me or somebody else will not make much difference. If they want to worship me they will worship me.

Have you pondered over the question: who are these people who ask you this question? They must be Hindus, Mohammedans, Christians, Jainas, Buddhists, Krishnamurti-ites. Who are these people? If they are so concerned about me, have they dropped Krishna? Have they dropped Mohammed? Have they dropped Buddha? If they are honest and sincere they would have dropped all the religions. But they go on carrying their Bibles, their Zendavestas, their Vedas, their Mahaviras, their Zarathustras, and still they are concerned only about me. What are their institutions? What is Hinduism? or Islam? or Jainism? or Communism for that matter?

Every institution is bound to be dead, only a man is alive. No institutions are ever alive. How can an institution be alive? By its very nature, it is going to be dead.

So next time these people ask you the question, you ask them: who are you? Do you belong to any institution, to any religion, to any theology, to any philosophy? If you belong, then you don't have the right to ask the question. And if you don't belong, then you will not need to ask the question: you will see the point that intelligent people will never fall for dead institutions. The unintelligent are bound to live in institutions – there is no way you can change the label. You are living in a thousand and one kinds of institutions.

What is marriage? – an institution. Only insane people live in institutions. Marriage is dead. What is your family, and what is your nation, and what is your race? – all institutions. This is a strange thing: people go on asking these questions without ever thinking that those questions are pointing toward themselves.

As far as I am concerned, I am not at all interested in the next moment. Even if this sentence remains incomplete, I will not make any effort to complete it. I will not even put a full point to it. I have no desire to dominate, but I cannot go on saying to people, "Don't worship me," because that is the way to create worship.

People are to be understood in their whole insane mechanisms. For example, Jesus says, "Blessed are the poor...for theirs is the Kingdom of God." Now, many, down these two thousand years have tried to be poor for the simple reason and motive so that they can attain to the Kingdom of God. Do you see the contradiction? "Blessed are the poor...for theirs is the Kingdom of God." What kind of poverty is this if it brings the Kingdom of God to you? Then this is a good incentive, a great motivation for greed. If Jesus was really right, he should have only said this, "Blessed are the poor because they are poor." Why make this statement: "...for theirs is the Kingdom of God"? Everybody wants to be of the Kingdom of God; everybody wants to possess eternal treasures. If one has to be poor and sacrifice for that, it is worth it.

People have been doing this all along. It is time that man start looking more clearly, more transparently – what has been told to him and what he has done.

People always misunderstand. When the master is alive they will not come to him, because when the master is alive they cannot be allowed to misunderstand. They will come to him only when he is no longer there, because a dead master can be controlled, manipulated.

Just a few days ago a so-called Jaina saint, Kanjiswami, died. He was worshipped by the Jainas so much that Jainas have been declaring that in the next circle of existence, in the next creation, he will be the first *teerthankara*, the first founder of Jainism, again.

When he died – I have seen the pictures, somebody sent me the pictures – the Jainas were trying to fix his posture, because a *teerthankara,* or a would-be *teerthankara,* should die in the lotus posture. They must have broken some of his bones. At least a dozen people were forcing his dead body into a certain yoga posture. Now, you cannot do this when a man is alive – he will go through a primal scream!

While he was alive he used to wear clothes. Now according to the Jainas, one attains to the ultimate freedom only when he dies naked. So they removed the clothes. Now, the corpse cannot prevent this. Clothes were removed, a lotus posture was fixed, and the followers are happy. This goes on happening.

A maid who seemed to enjoy her work gave notice one day without warning.

"Why do you wish to leave?" the lady of the house asked her. "Is anything wrong?"

"I just can't stand the suspense in this house a minute more," the maid replied.

"Suspense? What do you mean?"

"It's the sign over my bed. It says: 'Watch ye, for ye know not when the master cometh.'"

The moment the master is gone, you have only his words. Words can be manipulated, words can be interpreted, words can be colored and painted according to your prejudices. As far as I am concerned, it will be impossible – for many reasons it will be impossible.

First, I am a man who is consistently inconsistent. It will not be possible to make a dogma out of my words; anybody trying to make a creed or dogma out of my words will go nuts! You can make a dogma out of Mahavira – he is a very consistent man, very logical. You can make a philosophy out of Buddha – he is very mathematical. You can make a philosophy out of Krishnamurti – for fifty years he has been simply repeating the same thing again and again; you cannot find a single inconsistency in him. On the one hand he says "I am not your master, your guru. Don't depend on me." But in a subtle way he is creating the whole philosophy – which is so consistent, so utterly consistent – that anybody would like to be imprisoned in it, it is so sane.

It is impossible with me: I live in the moment, and whatsoever I am saying right now is true only for this moment. I have no reference with my past, and I don't think of the future at all. So my statements are atomic; they are not part of a system. You can make a dead institution only when a philosophy is very systematic, when there are no flaws, when no fault can be found in it, when all doubts are solved, all questions dissolved and you are given a ready-made answer to everything in life.

I am so inconsistent that it is impossible to create a dead institution around me, because a dead institution will need an infrastructure of a dead philosophy. I am not teaching you any doctrine, I am not giving you any principles. On the contrary, I am trying to take away all the philosophies that you have carried all along. I am destroying your ideologies, creeds, cults, dogmas – I am not replacing them with anything else. My process is of pure deconditioning. I am not trying to recondition you. I will leave you open.

Hence, you can see here, all my sannyasins are unique individuals. There is no certain pattern into which they have to fit themselves. There is no "should," no "should not"; there is no rigid structure, but only a liquidity. I am not giving you Ten Commandments; I am not giving you detailed information about how to live, because I believe in the individual and the individual's dignity and his freedom. I am sharing my vision – that is my joy – but it is not being shared in order that you should try to live up to it.

Krishnamurti goes on saying, "Don't follow me. Don't imitate me." On the other hand, when people don't follow him he becomes very irritated, annoyed. It is a little subtle. For example, he says, "Don't follow me," and people follow him. Then he becomes annoyed. If he is truly sincere, then you can say "Don't follow me," but if people want to follow you, who are you to prevent them? You have said your thing, now it is up to them to do or not to do. You are not their master; if they want to follow you, you cannot prevent them. If you prevent them, that means you are forcing them to follow your idea of not following.

He becomes very annoyed...

Just a few days ago he was in Mumbai, and I told my sannyasins, "Wherever he is, go there, and sit in the front rows." And the moment he saw the orange people he became unenlightened immediately, he started shouting!

Now, why this annoyance? There must be some deep desire to control. Now who are you to tell somebody not to wear orange? If somebody wants to wear orange, then it is his choice. A subtle strategy, a very indirect strategy to manipulate, to dominate, to possess...

I am simply sharing my vision, my joy. I am enjoying it, and whosoever wants to enjoy with me is welcome. Naturally, when I am gone there may be a few fools who will try to figure it out, to make a system, although I am making it almost impossible. But fools are fools. They can try to do the impossible.

Bertrand Russell has said that it is a strange fact of history that not a single religion has been founded by a man who had a sense of humor. In fact, to have a sense of humor and to create a religion is contradictory. Religions are created by sad people – very long faces, almost dead. Bertrand Russell is no longer alive, otherwise I would have told him, "Then come and see."

It may not have been so in the past, and I agree with him because Mahavira was serious, Jesus was serious, Mohammed was serious, Shankaracharya was serious... And Russell seems to be right that these sad people have created the dead institutions of all the religions.

But here something totally new is happening. I am not trying to create a religion; I cannot do it, because the very idea of creating a religion is ugly. I am releasing a sense of humor in you, a deep laughter in you. To me laughter is more sacred than prayer, dancing more spiritual than chanting mantras, loving existence far more cosmic than going to a church or to a temple. Becoming utterly nobody, a pure nothingness, is far more significant than becoming a saint. Innocence, a sense of humor, a joyous participation in life...you cannot create a dead institution around such tremendously alive experiences. A dead institution needs something dead to be made of. It is made out of the corpses of your saints. My whole approach is nonserious – sincere, but nonserious.

A salesman stopped at a small-town hotel and had difficulty getting a room.

He was about to leave when the clerk said, "I think I may be able to put you up. There are two beds up in room ten and one is occupied by a woman. But there is a screen around her bed and she is sleeping soundly. Just go to your bed quietly and everything will be fine."

The offer was quickly accepted. About twenty minutes later the salesman returned, greatly excited.

"Good heavens!" he cried. "The woman in the other bed is dead!"

"I know that," said the clerk, "but how the hell did you find out?"

People are curious, very curious.

You say: "I frequently hear a question being asked about the ashram... there is so much vitality here now and so much creativity with all these shows and music and fashions and crafts, as well as events happening abroad, that people are wondering what will happen when you are gone."

Tell those fools to come here when the thing is alive. When you see a beautiful rose flower you don't start thinking, "What will happen when the rose flower will wither away by evening? Its petals will fall and go back to the earth, to their original source – what will happen then?" You don't bother about it. You rejoice in the flower, you dance with the flower in the wind, in the rain, in the sun. You see a bird on the wing, soaring high toward the sky, toward the stars. You don't think, "What will happen when the bird is dead?" You enjoy it.

And, strangely, these are the people who create dead institutions, because when the bird is alive and singing and soaring high they are afraid to come close. When the bird is dead then they can make a beautiful golden cage – a temple, a synagogue, a church – and then they can worship. The dead bird is not dangerous.

These are the same people who are wondering what will happen who will create a dead institution. My people cannot create a dead institution – it is impossible. Those who have been in communion with me will have learned one thing absolutely, categorically: that life cannot be confined into institutions, and the moment you try to confine it into institutions you destroy it. So while I am alive they will celebrate. When I am gone they will still celebrate. They will celebrate my life, they will celebrate my death, and they will remain alive.

Remember, religions are created by guilty people, and I am not creating any guilt here.

There are certain mechanisms… If Jesus was not crucified, there would have been no Christianity at all. The real founder of Christianity is not Jesus Christ but the high priest of Jerusalem, the rabbi, and Pontius Pilate. These two persons, in conspiracy with Judas, created Christianity. This is the real "holy trinity"; Jesus Christ is just an excuse.

Crucify a man like Jesus and then you will never be able to forgive yourself, you will feel guilty. Your hands will look red with the blood of Jesus. Now, what should be done to remove those wounds, those guilt feelings? The only way is to move to the opposite: worship.

I am not sacrificing, hence there is no possibility of worshiping me. I am living joyously. Nobody need feel guilty for me, there is no reason at all. If I start living naked, if I start fasting, if I start moving barefoot on the roads, if I start begging for my food then I will create guilt, then I will create in you a subtle mechanism. Something will be triggered in you and finally you will find consolation only in worshiping me.

Mahavira is worshipped because he moved naked; tortured

himself, fasted. Buddha is worshipped because he was a king, renounced all his pleasures. I have not renounced anything. In fact, I was born a poor man and I live like a king. There is no need to worship me, because there is no need to compensate me. I am not creating any guilt in anybody. I am not torturing myself.

You can easily forgive yourself. There is no point in going on carrying guilt.

The whole idea of what will happen in the future is political. The politician is always concerned with the future.

A great politician had been bitten by a dog but did not give it much thought until he noticed that the wound was taking a remarkably long time to heal. Finally he consulted a doctor who took one look at it and ordered the dog brought in. Just as he had suspected, the dog had rabies. Since it was too late to give the patient serum, the doctor felt he had to prepare him for the worst.

The politician sat down at the doctor's desk and began to write. His physician tried to comfort him. "Perhaps it won't be so bad," he said. "You need not make out your will right now."

"I'm not making any will," replied the politician. "I'm just writing out a list of people I'm going to bite!"

I am not interested in the future at all. This moment is too much, too overwhelming. I am rejoicing in it. This is my way of life: to live moment to moment. I am not a prophet, I have not come here to determine the whole course of humanity in the future – that kind of bullshit does not appeal to me at all. Who am I to decide the whole course of humanity in the future? I am living my moment joyously; that's enough. And the people who will be coming, they will find their own ways to live. To suffer or to rejoice – it all depends on their intelligence.

I cannot determine anything, but my way of working is such that it is impossible to create a philosophy, a dogma, a creed, a church, absolutely impossible.

Eighty-five-year-old Will Jones hobbled down to the local bar to have a cold one and shoot the breeze with his friends. Mr. Jones was the talk of the town as he had recently married a beautiful nineteen-year-old girl. Several of the boys bought the old man a drink in an effort to get him to tell of his wedding night. Sure enough the old rascal fell right into their plans.

"My youngest son carried me in and lifted me on the bed with my young bride. We spent the night together and then my three other sons carried me off the bed."

The small circle of men scratched their heads and asked the old boy why it took his three other sons to take him off, when it only took his youngest boy to put him on.

Proudly he replied, "I fought them."

Live each moment totally.

You say to me, : "There is so much vitality here now..." The vitality is because we are living herenow, our whole vision is of herenow. We don't look beyond that because beyond that nothing exists; whatsoever comes is always now.

Time is an invention, now is a reality. So much creativity is happening for the simple reason that we have withdrawn from past and future.

Your whole energy remains blocked either in the past or in the future. When you withdraw all your energy from the past and the future a tremendous explosion happens. That explosion is creativity. This is only the beginning – every day, every moment, things are becoming intenser, more passionate. But we are not trying in any way to control the future.

I am not a prophet, neither I am a messiah. To me, the claims of Jesus Christ and people like that look childish: that they have come to deliver the whole of humanity from their sins. Krishna says in Gita, "Whenever religion will be lost, I will come back." To me, this is all crap. There is no need for anybody to come back; the people who will be here will take care of themselves.

I am preparing my people to live joyously, ecstatically. So when I am not here it won't make any difference to them. They will still live in the same way – maybe my death will bring them more intensity.

Death is always a beautiful background to make your life more intense. My ashram is never going to become a dead institution. And if it becomes so, it won't be *my* ashram.

You ask me, "When you leave your body will the ashram become a dead institution, and will you just become deified and forgotten?"

I am not leaving anything to anybody. I have declared myself *bhagwan*. I am not leaving anything to anybody. Why should I leave it to anybody? I know I am the Blessed One – and only I can know that, how can anybody else know it? I am trying to seduce my people to understand this immensity: that they are also the Blessed Ones. It is impossible to deify me – I have already done it! What else is there left for you? I don't depend on anybody.

Before I leave the world, one thing certainly I am going to do – it is private, so please don't tell it to anybody else... Before I leave the world, I am going to declare all of my sannyasins the Blessed Ones. Thousands of *bhagwans* all over the world! There will be no need to make any special nook and corner for me: I will be dissolved in my people. Just as you can taste the sea from any place and it is salty, you will taste any of my sannyasins and you will find the same taste: the taste of *bhagwan*, the taste of the Blessed One.

I am waiting for the right moment.

Once the new commune is established, all my sannyasins will be called *bhagwans*. Then it will be really a *"bhagwan* movement"!

The second question:

Osho,
If life is so beautiful, then what is the point of being enlightened and not being reborn?

There is no point at all. That's what I have been telling to you, but you don't listen. Your question shows that you have not listened. The question begins: "*If* life is so beautiful..." If's and but's won't do. If life is beautiful then you need not be enlightened. Life *is* beautiful, then there is no need to be enlightened.

Are you a Pollack or something?

A lady was looking in a bookstall for a gift for a sick Pollack friend.

When asked if she would like something religious, she replied, "Oh, no. My Pollack friend is well on the way to recovery!"

If you can drop that *if*, you will be on the way to recovery. But that *if* is there...I can see it sitting on you like a huge mountain.

I don't see any point in being enlightened. Things are perfectly beautiful as they are. But if you start with a hypothetical question then you have not tasted life. Drop the *if* and you are enlightened. There is not much in enlightenment. It is a simple recognition that "I have been unnecessarily chasing my own tail." The day you get it you stop chasing your tail. You just simply sit in the sun and take a sunbath.

A Pollack landowner had been wondering for quite a while about the quietness of his barnyard during the mid-day breaks. One day he decided to find out what was behind it all, and he stepped out discreetly and saw his farmhand crossing the yard with open pants and disappearing into the barn. The landowner called his servant back and asked him what was going on inside the barn.

"Well, sir, we've got quite a jolly game going on in there. The girls hide their heads in the hay and then have to guess who did it!"

"That sounds like fun," replies the Pollack landowner. "Can I join you?"

"I guess so," says the farmhand. "Your wife has been at it for six weeks already!"

You can join, but drop the *if*. Those who have dropped the *if*, they have already joined the game. The Buddhas and the Krishnas and the Zarathustras – they have joined the game just by dropping the *if*.

It is very difficult to drop *if's* and *but's* – the mind consists of them; these are the bricks of the mind. And all minds are Polack, remember.

The Pollack Pope was finally persuaded by his Cardinals to find a woman, so that he could better understand the problems of mankind.

"Well-a, okay," said the Pollack Pope, "but-a she's-a gotta have certain qualifications. First-a, she's-a gotta be blind, so she cannot see-a what-a I am-a doing to her. Second-a, she's-a gotta be deaf, so she cannot hear-a what I say-a. And third-a, she's-a gotta have-a the biggest tits-a in Italy!"

People are trying to play the game of life but with many conditions, and those conditions prevent them.

Life is a beautiful game if you don't have any conditions for it. If you can simply plunge into it with no *if's*, with no *but's;* then there is no need for enlightenment.

What is actually meant by enlightenment? – a relaxed, restful approach to life, a deep synchronicity with existence, an egoless communion with the whole.

A Pollack stripper goes to a theater manager for an audition. Before beginning her performance, she puts a big red apple in the middle of the stage and to the accompaniment of soft sexy music, she begins her number.

The music comes to a crescendo...she is almost naked. With a crash of cymbals and a roll of drums, to the gaping eyes of the theater manager, she leaps across the stage, does three impressive pirouettes and with one final crash of the drums dives down in the splits and lands on top of the big red apple.

When she gets up to bow, the apple has disappeared.

After a moment of deathly hush, the theater manager applauds her ecstatically.

"You will become famous all over the world. I will book you for the best theaters in Tokyo, London, Hamburg, New York and Paris."

"No! Paris no!" replies the stripper in a worried tone.

"Why not Paris?" asks the manager. "It's one of the best cities in the world for your number."

"No, not Paris! In Paris my mother does this number with a watermelon!"

The third question:

Osho,
What makes the fish jump out of the water?

Stephen Lyons, it is a strange question...it is fishy! Have you been a fish in your past life, or are you planning to be born as a fish in the future?

I don't know much about the fish and their minds, but I guess that they must be just like you: getting tired of the same ocean, the same water, the obvious. They must be jumping out of the water just to see what is beyond. They must be in search of enlightenment, nirvana. Or perhaps, trying to get out of the known, to have some taste of the unknown.

The Indian mythology is that the first incarnation of God happened in the form of a fish. That seems to be very relevant, because that's what biologists say: that life must have started in the ocean as a fish. Then compare... Even the fish is curious, inquiring. And there are millions of men who are not curious at all, not inquiring at all, who are living with stuffed ideas – borrowed rubbish from others – who are not explorers. The fish jumping out of the water shows you that you have fallen even below that.

A Christian remains a Christian, a Hindu remains a Hindu, a Mohammedan remains a Mohammedan – not only that, they brag. They are far worse than the most primitive form of life, the fish. One should inquire, one should explore. It is accidental that you are born a Hindu or a Mohammedan; it is not your destiny. Explore, jump out of the water, look around. There are millions of possibilities available, and the more you explore the more you are. The more you go into the unknown the more integrated you become. The challenge of the unknown is the most centering phenomenon in life.

Perhaps the fishes are jumping out of water just to listen to a few of my jokes.

Mrs. Cantor suspected her husband of playing around with the maid.

Having to spend a few days with her sick mother, she told her small son, Harvey, to keep an eye on Poppa and the maid.

As soon as she returned she asked, "Harvey, did anything happen?"

"Well," said the boy, "Poppa and the maid went into the bedroom and took off their clothes and..."

"Stop! Stop!" shouted Mrs. Cantor. "We will wait until Poppa comes home."

Poppa was met at the door by his irate wife, cringing maid and confused son. "Harvey, tell me what happened with Poppa and the maid," stormed Mrs. Cantor.

"As I told you, Ma," said Harvey, "Poppa and the maid went into the bedroom and took off their clothes."

"Yes! Yes! Go on, Harvey," said Mrs. Cantor impatiently, "what did they do then?"

Replied Harvey, "Why, Mother, they did the same thing you and Uncle Bernie did when Poppa was in Chicago."

So, when you see again a fish jumping out of the water, please tell a joke.

A pretty girl walked up to a tall handsome man.

"Ohhh," she sighed, "you have such big muscular arms!"

"Yes," he responded, making a fist with one hand. He then pointed with the other hand to his muscles and said, "Eight inches! I measured them this morning."

"Ohhh," said the girl with admiration, "and you have such a big beautiful chest!"

The man laughed, stretched his arms in the air, and said, "Thirty-five inches! I measured it this morning."

The girl was amazed. She looked down at him, pointed her finger at his cock and asked, "How long?"

"Two inches," he replied.

"Only?" the girl asked disappointed.

The he-man took a deep breath, looked at the girl and said, "Measured from the floor, of course!"

Can you make a religion out of my jokes? Can you make a dead institution out of my jokes? It is impossible.

The last question:

Osho,
There is no more bottle, no more you, no more I, only this drunken joy that makes my toes curl in ecstasy. But, Osho, what was the joke?

The ultimate joke, the only joke...

The official, Riko, once asked Nansen to explain to him the old problem of the goose in the bottle.

"If a man puts a gosling into a bottle," said Riko, "and feeds him until he is full-grown, how can the man get the goose out without killing it or breaking the bottle?"

Nansen gave a clap with his hands and shouted, "Riko!"

"Yes, Master," said the official with a start.

"See," said Nansen, "the goose is out."

This is the only ultimate joke in existence. You are enlightened! You are buddhas, pretending not to be, pretending to be somebody else. And my whole work here is to expose you.

The goose is out! You will make every effort to put it back into the bottle, because once the goose is out then you don't have any problems. Man knows only how to live with problems, he does not know how to live without problems, so he goes on putting the goose back into the bottle.

There is a beautiful poem of Rabindranath Tagore.

He says: I was searching for God for thousands of lives. I saw him…sometimes far away, close to a distant star. I rushed on. By the time I reached that place he had gone further ahead. It went on and on. Finally I arrived at a door, and on the door there was a signboard: "This is the house where God lives" – Lao Tzu House!

Rabindranath says, "I became very worried for the first time. I became very troubled. Trembling, I went up the stairs. I was just going to knock on the door and suddenly, like a flash, I saw the whole point. If I knock on the door and God opens the door, then what? Then everything is finished – my journeys, my pilgrimages, my great adventures, my philosophy, my poetry, all my longings of the heart – all is finished! It will be suicide.

"Seeing the point so crystal clear," Rabindranath says, "I removed my shoes from my feet, because getting back down the stairs may create some noise – he may open the door! Then what? And since the moment I reached the bottom of the steps I have not looked back. I have been running and running for thousands of years. I am still searching for God, although now I know where he lives. So I only have to avoid Lao Tzu House, and I can go on searching everywhere else for him. There is no fear…but I have to avoid that house. That house haunts me; I remember it perfectly. If by chance accidentally I enter into that house, then all is finished."

It is a beautiful insight.

Man lives in problems; man lives in misery. To live without problems, to live without misery, needs real courage.

I have lived without any problems for twenty-five years, and I know it is a kind of suicide. I simply go on sitting in my room doing nothing. There is nothing to do!

If you can allow so much silence to penetrate your very being, only then you will be able to leave the goose out of the bottle. Otherwise, for a moment maybe…again you will push the goose back into the bottle. That gives you an occupation; keeps you occupied, keeps you concerned, worried, anxious. The moment there are no problems, there is no mind. The moment there are no problems, there is no ego. The ego and the mind can exist only in the turmoil of problems.

As I see it, man creates problems to nourish his ego. If there are no real problems he will invent them. He is bound to invent them, otherwise his mind cannot function anymore.

This is my simple declaration: that *all* is divine. The trees and the rocks and the stones and the mountains and the stars – all are divine. The goose has never been in the bottle. It is only man who cannot live without problems who forces the goose into the bottle; and then he starts asking how to get it out. Then he makes impossible conditions: first, the bottle should not be broken, then the goose should not be killed.

Now the goose is big, it is filling the whole bottle. It is impossible to fulfill the conditions. Either the bottle has to be broken – that is not allowed; or the goose has to be killed – that is not allowed. You have to bring the goose out without killing it and without destroying the bottle. That is not possible, in the very nature of things. *Aes dhammo sanantano*: this *is* how life's law is, it is not possible. So man remains happy because it is not possible, so he can go on carrying the bottle.

I see you carrying the bottle with the goose… But the truth is that the bottle is only your imagination, fantasy, just made of the same stuff dreams are made of.

This is the most difficult thing for humanity to accept. Hence, so much opposition to me – because I am telling you that you are gods, that you are buddhas, that there is no other god than you. That is the most difficult thing to accept. You would like to be a sinner, you would like to be guilty, you would like to be thrown into hell; but you cannot accept that you are a buddha, the awakened one, because then all problems are solved. And when problems are solved, *you* start disappearing. And to disappear into the whole is the only thing worth doing, is the only thing of any significance.

What I am telling to you is not a teaching. This place is a device – this is a buddhafield. I have to take away things which you don't have, and I have to give you things which you already have. You need not be grateful to me at all, because I am not giving you anything new. I am simply helping you to remember. You have forgotten the language of your being.

I have come to recognize it: I have remembered myself. And since the day I remembered myself I have been in a strange situation: I feel compassion for you, and deep down I also giggle at you, because you are not *really* in trouble. You don't need compassion, you need hammering! You need to be hit hard on the head! Your suffering is bogus. Ecstasy is your very nature.

You are truth, you are love; you are bliss, you are freedom.

Enough for today.

about Osho

Osho's unique contribution to the understanding of who we are defies categorization. Mystic and scientist, a rebellious spirit whose sole interest is to alert humanity to the urgent need to discover a new way of living. To continue as before is to invite threats to our very survival on this unique and beautiful planet.

His essential point is that only by changing ourselves, one individual at a time, can the outcome of all our "selves" – our societies, our cultures, our beliefs, our world – also change. The doorway to that change is meditation.

Osho the scientist has experimented and scrutinized all the approaches of the past and examined their effects on the modern human being and responded to their shortcomings by creating a new starting point for the hyperactive 21ˢᵗ Century mind: OSHO Active Meditations.

Once the agitation of a modern lifetime has started to settle, "activity" can melt into "passivity," a key starting point of real meditation. To support this next step, Osho has transformed the ancient "art of listening" into a subtle contemporary methodology: the OSHO Talks. Here words become music, the listener discovers who is listening, and the awareness moves from what is being heard to the individual doing the listening. Magically, as silence arises, what needs to be heard is understood directly, free from the distraction of a mind that can only interrupt and interfere with this delicate process.

These thousands of talks cover everything from the individual quest for meaning to the most urgent social and political issues facing society today. Osho's books are not written but are transcribed from audio and video recordings of these extemporaneous talks to international audiences. As he puts it, "So remember: whatever I am saying is not just for you...I am talking also for the future generations."

Osho has been described by *The Sunday Times* in London as one of the "1000 Makers of the 20th Century" and by American author Tom Robbins as "the most dangerous man since Jesus Christ." *Sunday Mid-Day* (India) has selected Osho as one of ten people –

along with Gandhi, Nehru and Buddha – who have changed the destiny of India.

About his own work Osho has said that he is helping to create the conditions for the birth of a new kind of human being. He often characterizes this new human being as "Zorba the Buddha" – capable both of enjoying the earthy pleasures of a Zorba the Greek and the silent serenity of a Gautama the Buddha.

Running like a thread through all aspects of Osho's talks and meditations is a vision that encompasses both the timeless wisdom of all ages past and the highest potential of today's (and tomorrow's) science and technology.

Osho is known for his revolutionary contribution to the science of inner transformation, with an approach to meditation that acknowledges the accelerated pace of contemporary life. His unique OSHO Active Meditations™ are designed to first release the accumulated stresses of body and mind, so that it is then easier to take an experience of stillness and thought-free relaxation into daily life.

Two autobiographical works by the author are available:
Autobiography of a Spiritually Incorrect Mystic,
St Martins Press, New York (book and eBook)
Glimpses of a Golden Childhood,
OSHO Media International, Pune, India (book and eBook)

OSHO international meditation resort

Each year the Meditation Resort welcomes thousands of people from more than 100 countries. The unique campus provides an opportunity for a direct personal experience of a new way of living – with more awareness, relaxation, celebration and creativity. A great variety of around-the-clock and around-the-year program options are available. Doing nothing and just relaxing is one of them!

All of the programs are based on Osho's vision of "Zorba the Buddha" – a qualitatively new kind of human being who is able *both* to participate creatively in everyday life *and* to relax into silence and meditation.

Location
Located 100 miles southeast of Mumbai in the thriving modern city of Pune, India, the OSHO International Meditation Resort is a holiday destination with a difference. The Meditation Resort is spread over 28 acres of spectacular gardens in a beautiful tree-lined residential area.

OSHO Meditations
A full daily schedule of meditations for every type of person includes both traditional and revolutionary methods, and particularly the OSHO Active Meditations™. The daily meditation program takes place in what must be the world's largest meditation hall, the OSHO Auditorium.

OSHO Multiversity
Individual sessions, courses and workshops cover everything from creative arts to holistic health, personal transformation, relationship and life transition, transforming meditation into a lifestyle for life and work, esoteric sciences, and the "Zen" approach to sports and recreation. The secret of the OSHO Multiversity's success lies in the fact that all its programs are combined with meditation, supporting the understanding that as human beings we are far more than the sum of our parts.

OSHO Basho Spa

The luxurious Basho Spa provides for leisurely open-air swimming surrounded by trees and tropical green. The uniquely styled, spacious Jacuzzi, the saunas, gym, tennis courts...all these are enhanced by their stunningly beautiful setting.

Cuisine

A variety of different eating areas serve delicious Western, Asian and Indian vegetarian food – most of it organically grown especially for the Meditation Resort. Breads and cakes are baked in the resort's own bakery.

Night life

There are many evening events to choose from – dancing being at the top of the list! Other activities include full-moon meditations beneath the stars, variety shows, music performances and meditations for daily life.

Facilities

You can buy all of your basic necessities and toiletries in the Galleria. The Multimedia Gallery sells a large range of OSHO media products. There is also a bank, a travel agency and a Cyber Café on-campus. For those who enjoy shopping, Pune provides all the options, ranging from traditional and ethnic Indian products to all of the global brand-name stores.

Accommodation

You can choose to stay in the elegant rooms of the OSHO Guesthouse, or for longer stays on campus you can select one of the OSHO Living-In programs. Additionally there is a plentiful variety of nearby hotels and serviced apartments.

www.osho.com/meditationresort
www.osho.com/guesthouse
www.osho.com/livingin

MORE BOOKS AND EBOOKS BY OSHO MEDIA INTERNATIONAL

The God Conspiracy:
The Path from Superstition to Super Consciousness

Discover the Buddha: 53 Meditations to Meet the Buddha Within
Gold Nuggets: Messages from Existence

OSHO Classics
The Book of Wisdom: The Heart of Tibetan Buddhism.
The Mustard Seed: The Revolutionary Teachings of Jesus
Ancient Music in the Pines: In Zen, Mind Suddenly Stops
The Empty Boat: Encounters with Nothingness
A Bird on the Wing: Zen Anecdotes for Everyday Life
The Path of Yoga: Discovering the Essence and Origin of Yoga
And the Flowers Showered: The Freudian Couch and Zen
Nirvana: The Last Nightmare: Learning to Trust in Life
The Goose Is Out: Zen in Action
Absolute Tao: Subtle Is the Way to Love, Happiness and Truth

The Tantra Experience: Evolution through Love
Tantric Transformation: When Love Meets Meditation

Pillars of Consciousness (illustrated)
BUDDHA: His Life and Teachings and Impact on Humanity
ZEN: Its History and Teachings and Impact on Humanity
TANTRA: The Way of Acceptance
TAO: The State and the Art

Authentic Living

Danger: Truth at Work: The Courage to Accept the Unknowable
The Magic of Self-Respect: Awakening to Your Own Awareness
Born With a Question Mark in Your Heart

OSHO eBooks and "OSHO-Singles"

Emotions: Freedom from Anger, Jealousy and Fear
Meditation: The First and Last Freedom
What Is Meditation?
The Book of Secrets: 112 Meditations to Discover the Mystery Within

20 Difficult Things to Accomplish in This World
Compassion, Love and Sex
Hypnosis in the Service of Meditation
Why Is Communication So Difficult, Particularly between Lovers?
Bringing Up Children
Why Should I Grieve Now?: facing a loss and letting it go
Love and Hate: just two sides of the same coin

Next Time You Feel Angry...
Next Time You Feel Lonely...
Next Time You Feel Suicidal...

OSHO Media BLOG
http://oshomedia.blog.osho.com

for more information

www.**OSHO**.com

a comprehensive multi-language website including a magazine, OSHO Books, OSHO Talks in audio and video formats, the OSHO Library text archive in English and Hindi and extensive information about OSHO Meditations. You will also find the program schedule of the OSHO Multiversity and information about the OSHO International Meditation Resort.

http://OSHO.com/AllAboutOSHO
http://OSHO.com/Resort
http://OSHO.com/Shop
http://www.youtube.com/OSHO
http://www.Twitter.com/OSHO
http://www.facebook.com/pages/OSHO.International

To contact OSHO International Foundation:
www.osho.com/oshointernational,
oshointernational@oshointernational.com